FINANCIAL INSTITUTIONS AND SERVICES

FEDERAL FINANCIAL REPORTING

ELEMENTS AND CONSIDERATIONS

FINANCIAL INSTITUTIONS AND SERVICES

Additional books in this series can be found on Nova's website under the Series tab.

Additional e-books in this series can be found on Nova's website under the e-book tab.

FINANCIAL INSTITUTIONS AND SERVICES

FEDERAL FINANCIAL REPORTING

ELEMENTS AND CONSIDERATIONS

DENISE MAHONEY
EDITOR

nova publishers
New York

Additional color graphics may be available in the e-book version of this book.

Library of Congress Cataloging-in-Publication Data

ISBN: 978-1-62948-871-4

Published by Nova Science Publishers, Inc. † New York

CONTENTS

PREFACE

Federal financial reporting, defined here as the process of recording retrospective executive department-level financial and performance information, can provide both a snapshot of the government's financial health at a given moment in time, as well as an accounting of its financial performance over a particular time frame. Federal financial reports may help the federal government demonstrate accountability, provide information for policy formulation and planning, and be used to evaluate governmental performance. This book provides an overview of federal financial reporting; an understanding for the primary components of the annual financial report of the United States government; a citizen's guide to the 2012 financial report of the United States government; and provides an management report on improvements needed in controls over the preparation of the United States consolidated financial statements.

Chapter 1 – Federal financial reporting—defined here as the process of recording retrospective executive department-level financial and performance information—can provide both a snapshot of the government's financial health at a given moment in time, as well as an accounting of its financial performance over a particular time frame. Federal financial reports may help the federal government demonstrate accountability, provide information for policy formulation and planning, and be used to evaluate governmental performance. Multiple reports are required by law, and all are intended to permit users—Congress, the President, agency heads, program managers, and citizens—to see how the government raises, handles, and expends public money. Congress, in particular, may find the information in federal financial reports useful for oversight. The Budget and Accounting Procedures Act of 1950 was the first statute to require executive agencies to provide reports and information on their financial condition to the Secretary of the Treasury. The Chief Financial Officers Act of 1990 (CFO Act) mandates the preparation of audited annual financial statements for certain funds and accounts from a number of executive branch agencies, with 10 agencies selected to provide audited annual financial statements for all agency accounts. The latter provision was expanded to every agency covered under the CFO Act (commonly referred to as CFO agencies) in the Government Management Reform Act of 1994 (GMRA) and to every executive agency in the Accountability of Tax Dollars Act of 2002 (ATDA). In addition, the CFO Act requires the director of the Office of Management and Budget (OMB) to furnish an annual financial management status report and a government-wide five-year financial management plan, and GMRA requires the Secretary of the Treasury to provide government-wide annual consolidated financial statements to be audited by the Government Accountability Office (GAO). GAO has documented improvements to federal financial reporting since the enactment of the CFO Act. Demonstrable progress has been in evidence across numerous financial management indicators, including timeliness, consistency, and auditability. In FY2012, 21 of 24 CFO agencies received unqualified (clean) audit opinions on their annual financial statements, which means that their statements were free of material misstatements and accord with Generally Accepted Accounting Principles (GAAP). Challenges have persisted, though, both within agencies and government-wide. Unqualified overall audit opinions can obscure material weaknesses that underlie systematic financial management issues. In addition, two agencies—the Department of Homeland Security (DHS) and the Department of Defense (DOD)—have never received unqualified audit opinions, which signifies the persistence of financial problems at these agencies. Government-wide, the U.S. consolidated financial statements have received a disclaimer of opinion every year since they were first required under GMRA. GAO was unable to express an opinion on the FY2012 U.S. consolidated financial statements due to material weaknesses in internal control over financial reporting and other limitations on the scope of its work. Finally, federal financial statements may not provide readily understandable information to their multiple stakeholders. Congress has recently considered legislation relating to audits of federal financial statements. In the 113th Congress, Representative Lee has introduced legislation (H.R. 559) that would require a 5% reduction in a federal agency's discretionary budgetary authority for failure to produce an annual financial statement or failure to receive either an unqualified or qualified audit opinion on its annual financial statement. H.R. 559 was referred to the Committee on Oversight and

Government Reform and the Committee on Armed Services. The 112th Congress considered similar legislation, as well as legislation on audited annual financial statements at DOD and DHS, specifically. In the 112th Congress, Senator Coburn introduced the Audit the Pentagon Act, which would have mandated auditable financial statements by DOD for its FY2017 statements. The legislation also would have required DOD to provide a complete and validated statement of budgetary resources by FY2014. Congress also considered legislation to address problems at the Department of Homeland Security in the 112th Congress. The DHS Audit Requirement Target Act of 2012 (DART, 126 Stat. 1591) was signed into law on December 20, 2012. The DART Act directs DHS to obtain an unqualified audit opinion beginning with its FY2013 annual financial statements.

Chapter 2 – Similar to a corporation's annual report, the Consolidated Financial Report (CFR) is the federal government's general-purpose report of accountability to the American public on its finances. It is intended to

- provide an overall view of the annual financial results of operations and the financial position of the federal government, including long-term commitments and obligations;
- demonstrate accountability for the money the federal government raises through taxes and for spending money according to the laws and regulations that govern the federal government's budgets and financial operations;
- report on the federal government's operating performance, accounting systems, and internal control; and
- demonstrate the federal government's stewardship over its resources.

Chapter 3 – The Citizen's Guide (Guide) to the Fiscal Year (FY) 2012 Financial Report of the U.S. Government summarizes the current financial position and condition of the U.S. Government (See "Where We Are Now", p. ii) and discusses key financial topics, including fiscal sustainability (See "Where We Are Headed", p. v). This Guide and the Financial Report of the U.S. Government are produced by the U.S. Department of the Treasury in cooperation with the Office of Management and Budget (OMB). The Secretary of the Treasury, Deputy Director for Management of OMB, and Comptroller General of the United States at the Government Accountability Office (GAO) believe that the information discussed in this Guide is important to all Americans.

Chapter 4 – Treasury, in coordination with OMB, prepares the *Financial Report of the United States Government*, which contains the CFS. Since GAO's first audit of the fiscal year 1997 CFS, certain material weaknesses and other limitations on the scope of its work have prevented GAO from expressing an opinion on the CFS, exclusive of the Statements of Social Insurance (SOSI). Also, GAO was unable to express opinions on the 2012, 2011, and 2010 SOSI and 2012 and 2011 Statements of Changes in Social Insurance Amounts because of significant uncertainties, primarily related to the achievement of projected reductions in Medicare cost growth, reflected in these statements. As part of the fiscal year 2012 CFS audit, GAO identified material weaknesses and other control deficiencies in the processes used to prepare the CFS. The purpose of this chapter is to (1) provide details on new control deficiencies GAO identified related to the preparation of the CFS, (2) recommend improvements, and (3) provide the status of corrective actions taken by Treasury and OMB to address GAO's prior recommendations relating to the preparation of the CFS that remained open at the end of the fiscal year 2011 audit.

In: Federal Financial Reporting
Editor: Denise Mahoney

ISBN: 978-1-62948-871-4

Chapter 1

FEDERAL FINANCIAL REPORTING: AN OVERVIEW*

Garrett Hatch

SUMMARY

Federal financial reporting—defined here as the process of recording retrospective executive department-level financial and performance information—can provide both a snapshot of the government's financial health at a given moment in time, as well as an accounting of its financial performance over a particular time frame. Federal financial reports may help the federal government demonstrate accountability, provide information for policy formulation and planning, and be used to evaluate governmental performance. Multiple reports are required by law, and all are intended to permit users—Congress, the President, agency heads, program managers, and citizens—to see how the government raises, handles, and expends public money. Congress, in particular, may find the information in federal financial reports useful for oversight.

The Budget and Accounting Procedures Act of 1950 was the first statute to require executive agencies to provide reports and information on their financial condition to the Secretary of the Treasury. The Chief Financial Officers Act of 1990 (CFO Act) mandates the preparation of audited annual financial

* This is an edited, reformatted and augmented version of a Congressional Research Service Publication, CRS Report for Congress R42975, dated October 22, 2013.

statements for certain funds and accounts from a number of executive branch agencies, with 10 agencies selected to provide audited annual financial statements for all agency accounts. The latter provision was expanded to every agency covered under the CFO Act (commonly referred to as CFO agencies) in the Government Management Reform Act of 1994 (GMRA) and to every executive agency in the Accountability of Tax Dollars Act of 2002 (ATDA). In addition, the CFO Act requires the director of the Office of Management and Budget (OMB) to furnish an annual financial management status report and a government-wide five-year financial management plan, and GMRA requires the Secretary of the Treasury to provide government-wide annual consolidated financial statements to be audited by the Government Accountability Office (GAO).

GAO has documented improvements to federal financial reporting since the enactment of the CFO Act. Demonstrable progress has been in evidence across numerous financial management indicators, including timeliness, consistency, and auditability. In FY2012, 21 of 24 CFO agencies received unqualified (clean) audit opinions on their annual financial statements, which means that their statements were free of material misstatements and accord with Generally Accepted Accounting Principles (GAAP). Challenges have persisted, though, both within agencies and government-wide.

Unqualified overall audit opinions can obscure material weaknesses that underlie systematic financial management issues. In addition, two agencies—the Department of Homeland Security (DHS) and the Department of Defense (DOD)—have never received unqualified audit opinions, which signifies the persistence of financial problems at these agencies. Government-wide, the U.S. consolidated financial statements have received a disclaimer of opinion every year since they were first required under GMRA. GAO was unable to express an opinion on the FY2012 U.S. consolidated financial statements due to material weaknesses in internal control over financial reporting and other limitations on the scope of its work. Finally, federal financial statements may not provide readily understandable information to their multiple stakeholders.

Congress has recently considered legislation relating to audits of federal financial statements. In the 113th Congress, Representative Lee has introduced legislation (H.R. 559) that would require a 5% reduction in a federal agency's discretionary budgetary authority for failure to produce an annual financial statement or failure to receive either an unqualified or qualified audit opinion on its annual financial statement. H.R. 559 was referred to the Committee on Oversight and Government Reform and the Committee on Armed Services.

The 112th Congress considered similar legislation, as well as legislation on audited annual financial statements at DOD and DHS, specifically.

In the 112th Congress, Senator Coburn introduced the Audit the Pentagon Act, which would have mandated auditable financial statements by DOD for its FY2017 statements. The legislation also would have required DOD to provide a complete and validated statement of budgetary resources by FY2014. Congress also considered legislation to address problems at the Department of Homeland Security in the 112th Congress. The DHS Audit Requirement Target Act of 2012 (DART, 126 Stat. 1591) was signed into law on December 20, 2012. The DART Act directs DHS to obtain an unqualified audit opinion beginning with its FY2013 annual financial statements.

BACKGROUND

Federal financial reporting—defined here as the process of recording retrospective executive department-level financial and performance information—may provide both a snapshot of the government's financial health at a given moment in time, as well as an accounting of its financial performance over a given time frame. According to the Federal Accounting Standards Advisory Board (FASAB),[1] the committee that establishes accounting standards for federal entities,

> "Financial reporting" may be defined as the process of recording, reporting, and interpreting, in terms of money, an entity's financial transactions and events with economic consequences for the entity. Reporting in the federal government also deals with nonfinancial information about service efforts and accomplishments of the government, i.e., the inputs of resources used by the government, the outputs of goods and services provided by the government, the outcomes and impacts of governmental programs, and the relationships among these elements.[2]

Responsible stewardship of public money is integral to governmental accountability, and federal financial reports supply information that links stewardship to accountability. According to FASAB, "Because a democratic government should be accountable for its integrity, performance, and stewardship, it follows that the government must provide information useful to assess that accountability."[3] Reliable financial information may facilitate informed decision making, government management, and policy implementation. In addition, federal financial reports may make it easier to monitor waste, fraud, and abuse in federal programs.

Several types of federal financial reports are required by law. Each report presents a distinct array of financial information intended to permit various stakeholders—Congress, the President, agency heads, program managers, and citizens—to evaluate the federal government's performance relative to the collection and disbursement of public money. Congress, in particular, may utilize the information in federal financial reports for policy formulation and planning, programmatic decision making, and exercising oversight authority (**Figure 1**).

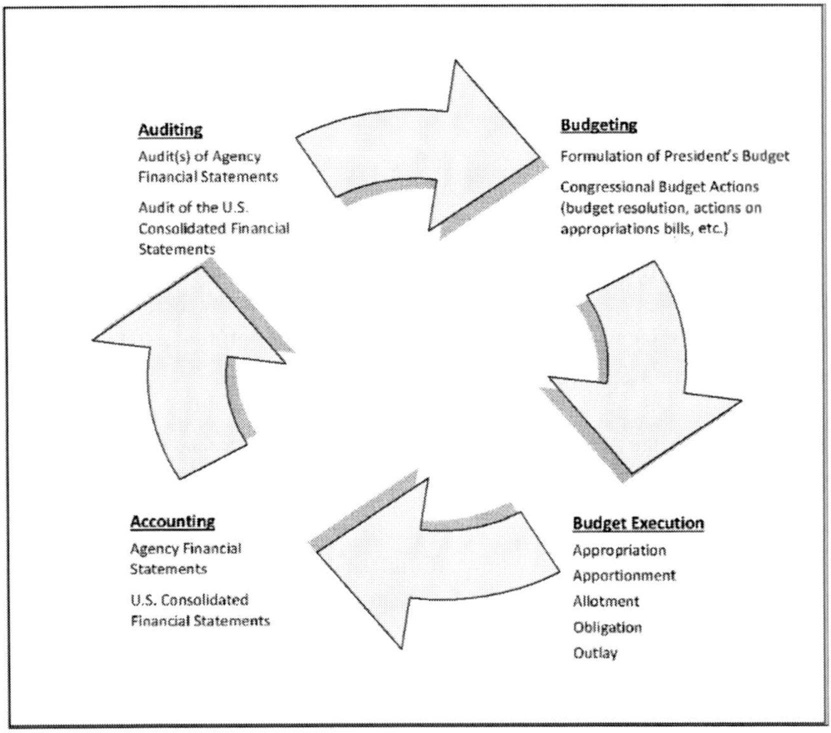

Source: Adapted from Gerald J. Miller, and Donijo Robbins, "Progressive Government Budgeting," in Frederic B. Bogui, ed., *Handbook of Governmental Accounting* (Boca Raton, FL: CRC Press, 2009), p. 75.

Figure 1. The Financial Management Cycle.

Objectives of Federal Financial Reporting

According to FASAB's "Authoritative Source of Guidance"[4] on generally accepted accounting principles (GAAP), there are four objectives of federal financial reporting: budgetary integrity, operating performance, stewardship, and systems and control.[5] FASAB defines a set of concepts for federal entities' general purpose financial reporting that meet these objectives.[6] Each statutorily mandated report addresses these objectives, albeit with varying degrees of emphasis.

Budgetary integrity. A federal financial report may satisfy the budgetary integrity objective if it provides information on "how budgetary resources have been obtained and used."[7] The Statement of Budgetary Resources, which must be included in agencies' annual financial statements, accords with the budgetary integrity objective by providing information on budgetary resources, obligations, and outlays.

Operating performance. A federal financial report may meet the operating performance objective by providing information on program and activity costs and accomplishments, as well as management of the reporting entity's assets and liabilities.[8] An example is the Statement of Net Cost required in agencies' annual financial statements. The Statement of Net Cost specifically addresses the operating performance objective[9] through its inclusion of information on program costs and the net cost of operations for the entire reporting entity, amongst other cost-related items.[10]

Stewardship. The stewardship objective concerns the government's financial position, defined as "a point-in-time snapshot of an entity's economic resources and the claims on those resources," and financial condition, which also conveys information about current financial health, as well as future expectations.[11] The *Financial Report of the United States Government*, the annual report on government-wide financial and performance information required by law, documents whether the government's financial position improved or worsened over the reporting period, indicates whether current budgetary resources are sustainable to meet future obligations, and presents other key indicators of the government's financial position and condition.[12] In so doing, it permits the reader to evaluate whether the government has been an effective steward of the nation's resources.

Systems and control. The systems and control objective states that federal financial reports should assist readers in determining whether financial management systems, internal accounting, and administrative controls are sufficient to satisfy the three previous objectives of budgetary integrity, operating performance, and stewardship.[13] Management's assertions about the effectiveness of internal controls[14]—for example, the "Management Assurances" statement in agencies' annual Performance and Accountability Reports (PARs)—fulfill the systems and control objective by documenting internal control over financial reporting.[15]

Audiences for Federal Financial Reports

FASAB identifies several audiences of federal financial reports: Congress, the President, agency heads, program managers, and citizens. Federal financial reports might be useful to each of these audiences for different reasons. In addition, certain aspects of federal financial reports might vary in degree of relevance for the stakeholder in question.

- Congress may use financial information contained in financial reports to conduct oversight of federal government programs and policies, consider policy alternatives, make decisions on the financing and execution of programs, monitor the effect of governmental financial commitments on the economy, and address persistent, long-standing accountability problems.
- The President and agency heads may use financial information to evaluate program performance, make program reauthorization decisions, and provide Congress with the resources necessary to perform its oversight function.
- Program managers may use financial information to ensure that resources are allocated properly, detect waste and inefficiency in program operations, and provide information that enables Congress, the President, and agency heads to monitor programs and activities.
- Citizens may use financial information to evaluate whether their elected and appointed representatives are responsible stewards of the public purse and gauge whether "the government is functioning economically, efficiently, and effectively."[16]

STATUTORY HISTORY AND CURRENT AUTHORITIES

Early Foundations of Modern Federal Financial Reporting

The U.S. Constitution serves as the foundation for federal financial reporting. Article I, Section 9, paragraph 7 states, "No Money shall be drawn from the Treasury, but in Consequence of Appropriations made by Law; and a regular Statement and Account of the Receipts and Expenditures of all public Money shall be published from time to time." This clause grants Congress the "power of the purse" but also requires a regular report of the receipts and expenditures of public money. In so doing, it links appropriations to accountability. Justice Joseph Story, who served on the U.S. Supreme Court from 1811-1845, stated, "Congress is made the guardian of this treasure; and to make their responsibility complete and perfect, a regular account of the receipts and expenditures is required to be published, that the people may know, what money is expended, for what purposes, and by what authority."[17] More recently, one Senator has observed of the appropriations-accountability link, "This is Congress's most important check on the executive branch in the Constitution's entire scheme of checks and balances. Congress cannot know that the executive branch is obeying the first part of the appropriations clause (spending) of the Constitution without confidence in the second (accountability)."[18]

Several measures subsequently established provisions for federal financial reporting that expanded on the constitutional mandate. In 1791, the U.S. House of Representatives approved a resolution on statements of receipts and expenditures. It resolved

> That it shall be the duty of the Secretary of the Treasury to lay before the House of Representatives, on the fourth Monday of October in each year, if Congress shall then be in session, or if not then in session, within the first week of the session next following the said fourth Monday of October, an accurate statement and account of the receipts and expenditures of all public moneys, down to the last day inclusively of the month of December immediately preceding the said fourth Monday of October, distinguishing the amount of the receipts in each State or District, and from each officer therein; in which statements shall also be distinguished the expenditures which fall under each head of appropriation, and shall be shown the sums, if any, which remain unexpended, and to be accounted for in the next statement, of each and every of such appropriation.[19]

Two pieces of legislation enacted during the Progressive Era further expanded on federal financial reporting requirements. The Dockery Act of 1894 required the Secretary of the Treasury to provide Congress with "an accurate, combined statement of the receipts and expenditures during the last preceding fiscal year of all public moneys."[20] Appropriations legislation for FY1908 legislative, executive, and judicial expenses contained a section that required the Secretary of the Treasury to include estimates of current and future public revenue and expenditures in its annual report to Congress.[21]

Finally, the Budget and Accounting Procedures Act of 1950 (BAPA) made significant changes to federal reporting requirements, and arguably was the foundation for present-day financial reporting.[22] BAPA authorized the Comptroller General, in consultation with OMB (formerly Bureau of the Budget) and Treasury, to "prescribe the principles, standards, and related requirements for accounting to be observed by each executive agency, including requirements for suitable integration between the accounting processes of each executive agency and the accounting of the Treasury Department."[23] Additionally, BAPA required agency heads to "establish and maintain systems of accounting and internal control designed to provide

(1) full disclosure of the financial results of the agency's activities;
(2) adequate financial information needed for the agency's management purposes;
(3) effective control over and accountability for all funds, property, and other assets for which the agency is responsible, including appropriate internal audit;
(4) reliable accounting results to serve as the basis for preparation and support of the agency's budget requests, for controlling the execution of its budget, and for providing financial information ... ; [and]
(5) suitable integration of the accounting of the agency with the accounting of the Treasury Department[.]"[24]

BAPA further required the Secretary of the Treasury to use agencies' financial information to prepare "such reports for the information of the President, the Congress, and the public as will present the results of the financial operations of the Government."[25]

THE CURRENT STATUTORY FRAMEWORK FOR FEDERAL FINANCIAL REPORTING

During the past two decades, Congress has further developed federal financial reporting through enactment of three statutes: (1) the Chief Financial Officers Act of 1990 (CFO Act), the Government Management Reform Act of 1994 (GMRA), and (3) the Accountability of Tax Dollars Act of 2002 (ATDA).

Chief Financial Officers Act of 1990

According to the Government Accountability Office (GAO, then the General Accounting Office), the CFO Act[26]

> is the most comprehensive and far-reaching financial management improvement legislation since the Budget and Accounting Procedures Act of 1950 was passed ... The CFO Act will lay a foundation for comprehensive reform of federal financial management. The act establishes a leadership structure, provides for long-range planning, requires audited financial statements, and strengthens accountability reporting.[27]

More specifically, the CFO Act

- established the Office of Federal Financial Management (OFFM) within OMB and designated a CFO in each executive department and major executive agency (subsequently known as CFO agencies);
- requires each CFO agency to prepare and audit annual financial statements for each revolving fund and trust fund and for accounts that performed substantial commercial functions;
- directed 10 agencies, including the Department of Agriculture, the General Services Administration, and the Department of the Army, to prepare audited financial statements for all of their agency accounts;[28] and
- requires the director of the OMB to produce an annual financial management status report and a government-wide, five-year financial management plan.[29]

Government Management Reform Act of 1994

GMRA[30] carried a range of provisions that sought to "improve the management of the Federal government through reforms to the management of human resources, financial management, and by other means."[31]

With regard to financial reporting, GMRA expanded the number of agencies covered by the CFO Act's reporting provisions from 10 to all CFO agencies (then 23).[32] The statute also requires

- all CFO agencies to prepare and submit audited financial statements for the previous year for all accounts and activities to the director of OMB;
- the Secretary of the Treasury to coordinate with the Director of OMB to prepare and submit an audited financial statement for the preceding fiscal year (i.e., all accounts and activities of the U.S. government) to the President and Congress beginning with financial statements prepared for FY1997; and
- GAO to audit these financial statements.

Accountability of Tax Dollars Act of 2002

To build upon this improvement, Congress enacted ATDA,[33] which

- further expanded the CFO Act's reporting requirements to cover all executive branch agencies to prepare and submit audited financial statements to OMB and the Congress; and
- permits OMB to exempt a non-CFO agency from this requirement if "the total amount of budget authority available to the agency for the fiscal year does not exceed $25,000,000; and ... the Director determines that requiring an annual audited financial statement for the agency with respect to the fiscal year is not warranted due to the absence of risks associated with the agency's operations, the agency's demonstrated performance, or other factors that the Director considers relevant."[34]

The Senate committee report on ATDA stated

> The financial reporting requirements of GMRA have prompted improvement in federal financial accountability. There has been steady progress at federal agencies toward achieving unqualified, or 'clean,' audit opinions. Only 6 of the 24 CFO Act agencies received clean opinions for fiscal year 1996, the first year GMRA was effective. For fiscal year 2001, 18 of the 24 agencies received clean opinions, and all of the CFO Act agencies met the statutory reporting deadline for the second year in a row.[35]

SELECTED FEDERAL FINANCIAL REPORTS

Each agency produces a range of reports on its financial activities. These reports are produced on different timetables and include different data and may be intended for either internal or external audiences.

Table 1 presents a selection of required annual federal financial reports. These reports provide data and analyses that are particularly useful for stakeholders wishing to examine agencies' financial performance in the previous year.

POSSIBLE OVERSIGHT ISSUES FOR CONGRESS

More than two decades have passed since the enactment of the first of the modern financial reporting statutes—the CFO Act. As recounted below, the congressional efforts to upgrade federal financial reporting have produced significant achievements; however, challenges remain.

Achievements in Federal Financial Reporting Since the CFO Act

Prior to the enactment of the CFO Act, GAO contended that agency-wide problems with internal control, poor executive management, and dated accounting systems were costing taxpayers billions of dollars.[36] Testifying before the House Committee on Government Operations, then- Comptroller

General Charles A. Bowsher stated, "In 1990, the federal government is operating with 1950s vintage accounting systems and concepts that just do not get the job done."[37] One bureau in a cabinet-level department, for example, had an unexpended balance recorded in its system that differed by over five times that reported by contractors and grantees.[38] Some financial managers attributed the prevalence of such poor financial information to the lack of an auditability requirement for executive departments.[39] Auditable financial statements, GAO has noted, form a pillar of the financial management structure insofar as they enhance the reliability of financial information and assist stakeholders in diagnosing problems preemptively.[40]

Low-quality financial information can have congressional implications. Writing prior to enactment of the CFO Act, GAO observed that financial statements did not disclose fully the federal government's financial commitments.[41] According to GAO, incomplete disclosures of financial information limited informed policymaking.[42] GAO recommended a permanent federal financial management structure that would ameliorate these problems and recommended that Congress pass legislation that would require, amongst other provisions, the preparation of auditable agency financial statements.[43]

Less than four years after the passage of the CFO Act, Comptroller General Bowsher noted its effect on federal financial reporting:

> The act's requirement for producing annual audited financial statements, in particular, is demonstrating its value in many important ways, including better highlighting the agencies' true financial conditions. Audited financial statements have also been integral to identifying management inefficiencies and weaknesses and highlighting gaps in safeguarding the government's assets and possible illegal acts. Additionally, the CFO Act financial audits have identified actual and potential savings of hundreds of millions of dollars.[44]

Further improvements have built on these initial results, with demonstrable progress across numerous financial management indicators, including timeliness, consistency, and auditability.

Table 1. Selected Federal Financial Reports: Authorities and Requirements

Report	Authorities	Submitted From	Submitted To	Submission Date	Contains
Agency Financial Report	CFO Act (1990) GMRA (1994) ATDA (2002)	Agency head	Congress GAO OMB Treasury (Main / FMS)	November 15	Agency Head Message Management's Discussion and Analysis (MD&A) Financial Section[a] Other Accompanying Information (OAI)
Financial Report of the United States Government	GMRA (1994)	Secretary of the Treasury (coordinates with Director of OMB)	Congress President	December 15	Citizen's Guide Management's Discussion and Analysis (MD&A) Financial Statements Notes to Financial Statements Supplemental Information Stewardship Information
Federal Financial Management Report[b]	CFO Act (1990)	Director of OMB	Congress	January 31	Description of financial management in the executive branch Summary of agencies' audited financial statements Government-wide 5-year financial management plan

Source: Compiled by CRS from several sources: relevant statutory authorities (CFO Act, GMRA, and ATDA); Office of Management and Budget, *Financial Reporting Requirements*, August 3, 2012, at http://www.whitehouse.gov/sites/default/files/omb/assets/omb/circulars/a136/a136_revised_2012.pdf; Department of the Treasury, *Financial Report of the United States Government* (selected years), http://www.fms.treas.gov/fr/ index.html; Government Accountability Office, *Understanding the*

Primary Components of the Annual Financial Report of the United States Government, GAO-09-946SP, September 2009, at http://www.gao.gov/assets/80/77222.pdf.

Notes: While the submission date varies for the different reports, each is required annually.

a. The Financial Section must contain: a CFO Letter, an Auditor's Report, and Financial Statements and Notes. Financial Statements and Notes consists of the principal financial statements—Balance Sheet, Statement of Net Cost, Statement of Changes in Net Position, Statement of Budgetary Resources, Statement of Custodial Activity (when applicable), Statement of Social Insurance (when applicable), and Statement of Changes in Social Insurance Amounts (when applicable)—and notes to financial statements, required supplementary information (RSI), and required supplementary stewardship information (RSSI). Office of Management and Budget, *Financial Reporting Requirements*, August 3, 2012, at http://www.whitehouse.gov/ sites/default/files/omb/assets/omb/ circulars/a136/a136_revised_2012.pdf.

b. The most recent Federal Financial Management Report that CRS was able to locate is the 2009 report.Office of Management and Budget, *Federal Financial Management Report 2009*, at http://www.whitehouse.gov/ sites/default/files/omb/ assets/ about_omb/2009_fin.pdf.

The CFO Act mandated the production of timely financial information. Overall, agencies have accelerated the delivery of their annual auditable financial statements from the statutorily required five months (following the close of the fiscal year) to the current time frame of 45 days from the end of the fiscal year.[45] According to a joint report in 2011 from the Chief Financial Officers (CFO) Council and the Council of Inspectors General on Integrity and Efficiency (CIGIE), the financial reporting requirements in the CFO Act[46] have translated into higher quality and more consistent financial information, which has "provided increasing levels of credibility and confidence in government finances."[47] In FY2012, 21 of 24 CFO agencies received unqualified audit opinions on their annual financial statements. As shown in **Figure 2**, the number of CFO agencies per year with unqualified audit opinions has steadily increased over time, from 6 in FY1996 to 13 in FY1999 to 18 in FY2005 to the current high of 21. Unqualified (clean) opinions[48] on financial statements are indicators of strong financial management.[49]

Ongoing Challenges

The CFO Act, as amended by GMRA and ATDA, established a legislative framework that enhanced federal financial reporting, though several challenges have persisted, both at the agency level and government-wide. In addition, federal financial statements may not provide readily understandable information to their multiple stakeholders.

Financial Reporting Issues Within the CFO Agencies

Across the CFO agencies, the increase in numbers of unqualified audit opinions reflects the general trend over time (**Figure 2**), but these overall opinions may be only partially revealing. Unqualified overall audit opinions can obscure material weaknesses that underlie systematic financial management issues. In addition, two agencies—the Department of Homeland Security (DHS) and the Department of Defense (DOD)—have never received unqualified audit opinions, which signifies the persistence of financial problems at these agencies.[50]

Material Weaknesses

Some agencies have received unqualified overall audit opinions despite auditor-identified financial material weaknesses[51] that would not necessarily affect an agency's overall audit opinion but could signal costly underlying financial management issues regardless.[52] GAO has observed that "[m]any CFO Act agencies have obtained clean or unqualified audit opinions on their financial statements, but the underlying agency financial systems and controls still have some serious problems."[53] For example, the Department of Labor (DOL) received an unqualified audit opinion on its FY2011 consolidated financial statements, but the auditor's report still identified three material weaknesses:

- lack of sufficient controls over financial reporting;
- lack of sufficient controls over budgetary accounting; and
- lack of sufficient security controls over key financial and support systems.[54]

The auditor cited one case in which differences between general ledger transactions in DOL's accounting and reporting system and the consolidated trial balance for several general ledger accounts ranged from $30 billion to $47 billion for each account.[55] In general, OMB has suggested that as material weaknesses increase, so too does the likelihood of a significant misstatement in financial information.[56] According to OMB, unreliable financial information can inhibit program management and policy implementation.[57]

Financial Reporting Problems at DHS and DOD

Neither DHS nor DOD has ever achieved an unqualified audit opinion.[58] After eight years of disclaimers, though, DHS received a qualified audit opinion on its FY2011 annual financial statements.[59] The qualified audit opinion represented an improvement over the preceding disclaimers in that most of the line items on DHS's balance sheet were materially correct for the first time since FY2003.[60] DHS's FY2012 annual financial statements also received a qualified opinion.[61] DHS has stated that its next financial management objective is progress toward an unqualified audit opinion.[62] In order to accomplish this goal, DHS indicated that it would use risk assessments to identify and correct material weaknesses and deficiencies; implement a plan to modernize its core financial management system; establish standard business practices and internal controls, as well as implement a standard line of accounting; and retroactively obtain a clean, full-scope audit opinion on its FY2012 financial statements.[63]

Unlike DHS, DOD's current objective is auditability. Its annual financial statements have received a disclaimer of opinion since 1997, the first year in which department-wide annual audited financial statements were required.[64]

At a House hearing on financial management at DOD, Daniel Blair, the deputy inspector general for auditing at DOD, identified data quality, internal controls, and financial systems as three impediments to auditability.[65] Between FY2007 and FY2011, DOD's Office of Inspector General (OIG) issued 89 reports citing data quality problems.[66] Deputy Inspector General Blair described one example of a data quality issue in which DOD did not provide reliable information to Congress on the costs of Guam realignment for calendar year 2009—obligations were understated by over 10%, and expenditures were overstated by over 35%.[67] Poor internal controls have also had financial repercussions, according to Deputy Inspector General Blair.[68] In one example, Army Commercial Vendor Services incorrectly coded domestic contractors as foreign and then failed to file federal information returns to the Internal Revenue Service (IRS) for approximately 316 of the incorrectly coded payments in the amount of $351.92 million.[69] The OIG identified 13 areas of material weakness in DOD's financial reporting for FY2012.[70] Among the issues with financial systems is the Logistics Modernization Program, the Army Working Capital Fund's system for achieving auditable financial statements.[71] According to a 2011 OIG report, the Logistics Modernization Program was in development for 10 years and cost $1.1 billion, yet did not produce a system that was compliant with the U.S. Standard General Ledger.[72]

While the goal for DOD is auditability, auditability is not an end unto itself.[73] According to Deputy Inspector General Blair, auditable financial statements indicate improvement to the three impediments to auditability—data quality, internal controls, and financial systems.[74] The deputy inspector general noted that improvements in these three areas would permit DOD to provide accurate and timely financial information.[75] In the absence of reliable financial information, DOD is vulnerable to waste, fraud, and abuse. One GAO report states that

> DOD financial management has been on GAO's high-risk list since 1995 and, despite several reform initiatives, remains on the list today. Pervasive deficiencies in financial management processes, systems, and controls, and the resulting lack of data reliability, continue to impair management's ability to assess the resources needed for DOD operations; track and control costs; ensure basic accountability; anticipate future costs; measure performance; maintain funds control; and reduce the risk of loss from fraud, waste, and abuse. DOD spends billions of dollars each year to maintain key business operations intended to support the warfighter, including systems and processes related to the management of contracts, finances, supply chain, support infrastructure, and weapon systems

> acquisition. These operations are directly impacted by the problems in financial management. In addition, the long-standing financial management weaknesses have precluded DOD from being able to undergo the scrutiny of a financial statement audit.[76]

Congress has had a sustained interest in financial management problems at DOD. Reliable financial information helps Congress "distinguish between necessary budget cuts and cuts that would harm our troops and damage military readiness."[77] Various House and Senate committees have held hearings on the issue, and the House Armed Services Committee convened an oversight panel in the 112th Congress to perform a comprehensive review of DOD's financial management system. The House Armed Services Committee Panel on Defense Financial Management and Auditability Reform evaluated DOD's financial management challenges and plans for audit readiness and recommended courses of action in these areas.[78] The severity of the financial management problems at DOD extend beyond the agency level to have government-wide implications—GAO has identified the financial management problems at DOD as a barrier to auditing the U.S. consolidated financial statements, as discussed in the next section.

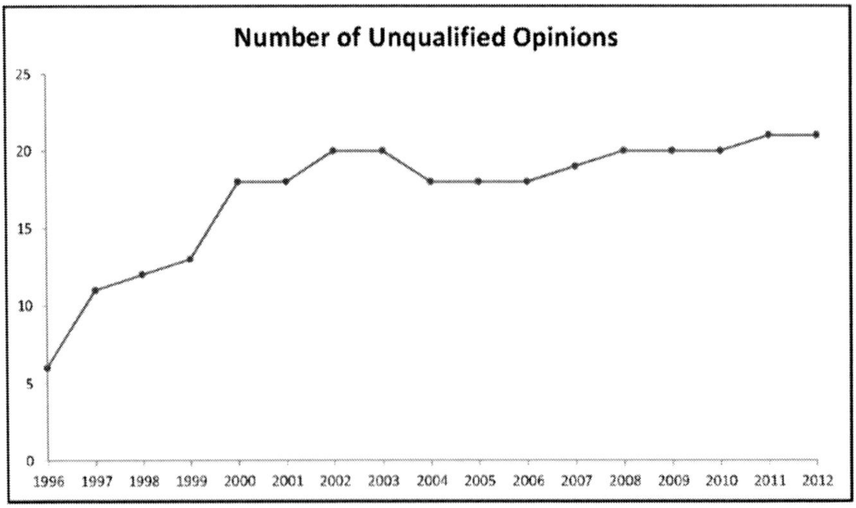

Source: Compiled by CRS from agency data.

Figure 2. Agency Unqualified (Clean) Audits.

Government-Wide Financial Reporting Issues

Government-wide, the U.S. consolidated financial statements[79] have received a disclaimer of opinion every year since they were first required under GMRA.[80] GAO was unable to express an opinion on the FY2012 U.S. consolidated financial statements due to material weaknesses in internal control over financial reporting and other limitations on the scope of its work.[81] The Comptroller General's transmission letter in the FY2012 *Financial Report of the United States Government* stated,

> While significant progress has been made in improving federal financial management since the federal government began preparing consolidated financial statements 16 years ago, three major impediments continued to prevent us from rendering an opinion on the federal government's accrual-based consolidated financial statements over this period: (1) serious financial management problems at DOD that have prevented its financial statements from being auditable, (2) the federal government's inability to adequately account for and reconcile intragovernmental activity and balances between federal agencies, and (3) the federal government's ineffective process for preparing the consolidated financial statements.[82]

These three enduring issues have continued to mitigate GAO's ability to render an opinion on the U.S. government's consolidated financial statements.[83] For FY2012, GAO identified several other underlying material weaknesses in internal control over financial reporting. GAO stated that the federal government could not

- determine whether property, plant, and equipment (PPE), primarily held by DOD, were properly reported;
- estimate or adequately support amounts reported for certain liabilities;
- support significant portions of the reported net cost of operations; and
- identify and resolve or explain material differences between certain components of the budget deficit and related amounts reported in federal entities' financial statements.[84]

According to GAO, the limitations that preclude it from expressing an opinion on the U.S. financial statements carry consequences. The material weaknesses identified by GAO inhibit the federal government in safeguarding its assets and recording its transactions correctly, as well as in measuring the full cost and performance of programs and activities.[85] They also diminish the reliability of information that would permit the federal government to operate efficiently and effectively.[86]

GAO found four additional material weaknesses beyond those that contributed to its disclaimer of opinion on the U.S. consolidated financial statements. These material weaknesses are improper payments,[87] information security control deficiencies, tax collection issues, and problems associated with federal grants management.[88]

GAO provides recommendations for resolving weaknesses in the U.S. consolidated financial statements. The recommendations, which may be issued in a separate management report, are tracked over time so that it is possible to determine which have been implemented and which have not. In its most recent management report, GAO noted that at the end of FY2011, there were 48 prior year recommendations that had yet to be implemented.[89] Of those, 31 remained open through the end of FY2012, including 14 that were first identified in FY2002.[90] The chapter identifies steps being taken to implement the recommendations.

Accessibility of Federal Financial Reports

Federal financial statements may not provide readily understandable information to their multiple stakeholders. According to the 2011 joint report prepared by the CFO Council and CIGIE, the ability to analyze financial statements requires specialized knowledge:

> Although the information contained in financial statements and Annual Performance Reports for the CFO Act agencies is robust, many believe that there is limited demand for this information outside of government, perhaps due to its technical nature, seeming complexity, and granular characteristics. Analyzing financial statements requires an in-depth understanding of government accounting principles, and most financial and performance reports contain details that may only appeal to the financial management community. In the continuing quest to improve government financial reports and ensure data accuracy, the financial management community should increase efforts to make financial information more relevant to all of its stakeholders, including decision-makers, program managers, and the public.[91]

For example, the various federal financial reports use similar terms (e.g., "cost," "net cost," etc.) but the definitions of these terms and the relationships between them and the accompanying financial figures conveyed can be difficult to discern to non-expert stakeholders (**Figure 3**). The Federal Accounting Standards Advisory Board established a task force on the financial reporting model in April 2010.[92] The task force reported that the government-wide financial report was difficult to navigate, even for task force members.[93] FASAB's user needs study[94] found that federal executives and managers, as well as citizens, found some difficulty in understanding information in financial reports—the prevailing belief was that financial reports were intended for accountants or economists.[95]

In addition, some have suggested that federal financial reports are not necessarily accessible to Congress. A survey of 239 federal financial management executives and managers indicated that the majority of respondents "believed federal financial statements cost too much to prepare and audit while delivering little useful information to government decision makers."[96] In a House subcommittee hearing on financial information in the federal government, Representative Edolphus Towns appeared to concur. He stated:

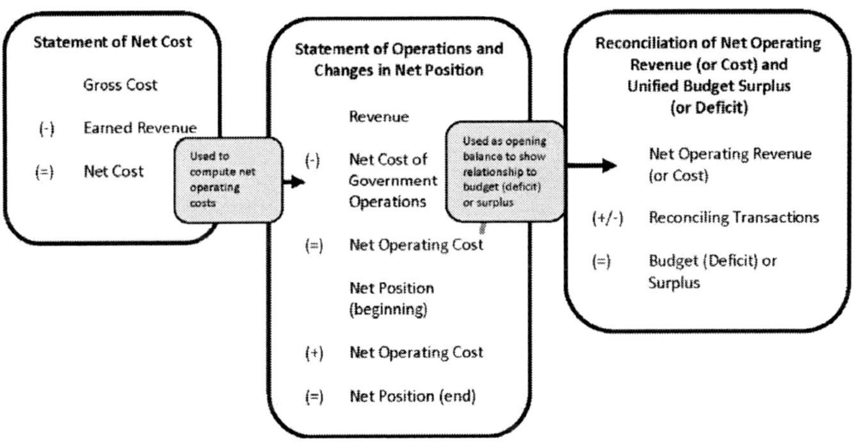

Source: Created by CRS based upon U.S. Department of the Treasury, "How the Federal Government's Financial Statements are Related to Each Other," *2006 Financial Report of the United States Government*, December 15, 2006, p. 12, at http://www.gao.gov/financial/fy2006/fy06finanicalrpt.pdf.

Figure 3. Example of the Relationship Between Terms in Different Federal Financial Reports.

> [W]hen it comes to interpreting the actual documents, too much complex information can lead to confusion. Too little information can be misleading.... From our experience, we know that understanding federal government financial statements and reports can be difficult, even for the experts. We need to have more readily available, simplified financial information in order to help both us here in the legislative branch, as well as the public.[97]

Congress requires tractable information to address issues as they arise.[98] Specifically, accessible information permits better understanding of government operations, serves as a shared platform from which policy positions may be established, affords an historical perspective on budgets and spending, allows comparison of agencies' fiscal results relative to budgets, and permits the performance of program evaluations.[99]

RECENT LEGISLATION

Congress has recently considered legislation relating to audits of federal financial statements. In the 113th Congress, Representative Barbara Lee has introduced legislation (H.R. 559) that would require a 5% reduction in a federal agency's discretionary budgetary authority for failure to produce an annual financial statement or failure to receive either an unqualified or qualified audit opinion on its annual financial statement. The 112th Congress considered similar legislation, as well as legislation on audited annual financial statements at DOD and DHS, specifically.

Audit the Pentagon Act

In the 112th Congress, Senator Tom Coburn introduced the Audit the Pentagon Act (S. 3487). S. 3487 would have mandated auditable financial statements by DOD for its FY2017 statements. Specifically, this legislation would have amended Section 1003 of the National Defense Authorization Act for Fiscal Year 2010 (2010 NDAA, P.L. 111-118). The 2010 NDAA required DOD's Chief Management Officer (CMO), in consultation with the Under Secretary of Defense (Comptroller), to ensure that its financial statements are validated as ready for audit no later than September 30, 2017.[100] S. 3487 differed from the 2010 NDAA in that it would have required the statements to be auditable, not just validated as ready for audit.[101]

The legislation also would have required DOD to provide a complete and validated statement of budgetary resources by FY2014. Failure to obtain an unqualified opinion on its FY2017 financial statements would have resulted in (1) the cessation of authorities on reprogramming and availability of funds authorized under the act, (2) a prohibition of expenditures of funds for major defense acquisition program activities beyond Milestone B,[102] and (3) a reorganization of the CMO position. S. 3487 was referred to the Senate Committee on Armed Services and was not enacted by the 112th Congress.

Representative Lee introduced companion legislation (H.R. 6528) in the House on September 21, 2012. H.R. 6528 differed from the Senate version in that it did not amend the auditability requirement. It would have imposed a 5% reduction in the discretionary budgetary authority of any agency required to produce an annual auditable financial statement that failed to (1) submit a financial statement for the previous fiscal year or (2) obtain either an unqualified or qualified audit opinion by an independent external auditor. The bill excluded from reduction accounts for military, reserve, and National Guard personnel and the Defense Health Program Account of DOD. In addition, the President would have been permitted to waive the reduction in discretionary budget authority if it jeopardized national security or members of the Armed Forces in combat. H.R. 6528 was not enacted by the 112th Congress.

In the 113th Congress, Representative Lee introduced the Audit the Pentagon Act of 2013 (H.R. 559).[103] It was referred to the Committee on Oversight and Government Reform and the Committee on Armed Services. H.R. 559 is nearly identical to the legislation proposed in the 112th Congress.[104]

DHS Audit Requirement Target Act

Congress also considered legislation to address problems at the Department of Homeland Security in the 112th Congress. Senator Scott Brown introduced the DHS Audit Requirement Target Act (DART, S. 1998) on December 15, 2011. Representative Todd Platts introduced the House version of the bill on June 8, 2012. Unlike the Audit the Pentagon Act, the purpose of the DART Act is not auditability. The DART Act directs DHS to obtain an unqualified audit opinion beginning with its FY2013 annual financial statements. In addition, the legislation requires DHS to provide Congress with its plan for meeting the deadline and for achieving better financial management. Congress instituted this requirement for the purposes of enhanced monitoring and oversight.[105] The DART Act of 2012 (126 Stat. 1591) was signed into law on December 20, 2012.[106]

APPENDIX. AGENCIES AND FEDERAL FINANCIAL REPORTING

Executive Departments and Agencies Subject to the CFO Act (CFO Agencies) Required to Prepare Financial Statements	
Department of Agriculture	Department of Transportation
Department of Commerce	Department of the Treasury
Department of Defense	Department of Veterans Affairs
Department of Education	Agency for International Development
Department of Energy	Environmental Protection Agency
Department of Health and Human Services	General Services Administration
Department of Homeland Security	National Aeronautics and Space Administration
Department of Housing and Urban Development	National Science Foundation
Department of the Interior	Nuclear Regulatory Commission
Department of Justice	Office of Personnel Management
Department of Labor	Small Business Administration
Department of State	Social Security Administration
Executive Agencies Subject to ATDA Required to Prepare Financial Statements	
Advisory Council on Historic Preservation	Japan-U.S. Friendship Commission
African Development Fund	Marine Mammal Commission
Appalachian Regional Commission	Merit Systems Protection Board
Architectural and Transportation Barriers	Morris K. Udall Scholarship and Excellence in
Compliance Board	National Environmental
Armed Forces Retirement Home	Policy Foundation
Barry Goldwater Scholarship and Excellence in Education Fund	National Archives and Records Administration
Broadcasting Board of Governors	National Capital Planning Commission

Central Intelligence Agency	National Commission on Libraries and Information Science
Chemical Safety and Hazard Investigation Board	National Council on Disability
Christopher Columbus Fellowship Foundation	National Credit Union Administration
Commission on Civil Rights	National Endowment for the Arts
Commission of Fine Arts	National Endowment for the Humanities
Commission for the Preservation of America's	National Labor Relations Board
Heritage Abroad	
Committee for Purchase from People Who Are	National Mediation Board
Blind or Severely Disabled	
Commodities Futures Trading Commission	National Transportation Safety Board
Consumer Product Safety Commission	Nuclear Waste Technical Review Board
Court Services and Offender Supervision Agency for DC	Occupational Safety and Health Review Commission
Defense Nuclear Facilities Safety Board	Office of Government Ethics
Delta Regional Authority	Office of Navajo and Hopi Indian Relocation Commission
Denali Commission	Office of Special Counsel
Equal Employment Opportunity Commission	Peace Corps
Farm Credit Administration	Presidio Trust
Farm Credit System Insurance Corporation	Railroad Retirement Board
Federal Communications Commission	Securities and Exchange Commission
Federal Election Commission	Selective Service System
Federal Financial Institutions Examination Council Appraisal Subcommittee	Smithsonian Institution (SI)
Federal Housing Finance Board	SI/John F. Kennedy Center for the Performing Arts
Federal Labor Relations Authority	SI/National Gallery of Arts
Federal Mediation and Conciliation Service	SI/Woodrow Wilson International Center for Scholars

Federal Mine Safety and Health Review Commission	Trade and Development Agency
Federal Retirement Thrift Investment Board	U.S. Court of Appeals for Veterans Claims
Federal Trade Commission	U.S. Holocaust Memorial Museum
Harry S. Truman Scholarship Fund	U.S. Interagency Council on Homelessness
Institute of American Indian and Alaska Native Culture and Arts Development	U.S. International Trade Commission
Institute of Museum and Library Services	Vietnam Education Foundation
Inter-American Foundation	White House Commission on the National Moment of Remembrance
James Madison Memorial Fellowship Foundation	
Government Corporations Required to Prepare Financial Statements	
Commodity Credit Corporation	Government National Mortgage Association
Community Development Financial Institutions Fund	Millennium Challenge Corporation
Corporation for National and Community Service	National Credit Union Administration Central Liquidity Facility
Export-Import Bank of the United States	Overseas Private Investment Corporation
Federal Crop Insurance Corporation	Pension Benefit Guaranty Corporation
Federal Deposit Insurance Corporation	Rural Telephone Bank
Federal Home Loan Banks	Resolution Funding Corporation
Federal Housing Administration Fund	Saint Lawrence Seaway Development Corporation
Federal Prison Industries, Incorporated	Tennessee Valley Authority
Financing Corporation	

Source: Constructed from Appendix A, Appendix C, and Appendix D of Office of Management and Budget, *Audit Requirements for Federal Financial Statements*, OMB Bulletin No. 07-04, September 4, 2007, pp. 33, 35-37, at http://www.whitehouse.gov/sites/default/files/omb/assets

End Notes

[1] The Federal Accounting Standards Advisory Board was established in 1990 by the Government Accountability Office (then the General Accounting Office), U.S. Department of the Treasury, and the Office of Management and Budget. Federal Accounting Standards Advisory Board, "The History of FASAB," webpage, at http://www.fasab.gov/about/ our-history/the-history-of-fasab/.

[2] Federal Accounting Standards Advisory Board, "SFFAC 1," in *FASAB Handbook of Federal Accounting Standards and Other Pronouncements, as Amended* (Washington, DC: 2011), p. 10, at http://www.fasab.gov/pdffiles/ 2011_fasab_handbook.pdf. SFFAC is an acronym for Statement of Federal Financial Accounting Concepts.

[3] Ibid., p. 21.

[4] Federal Accounting Standards Advisory Board, "Authoritative Source of Guidance," at http://www.fasab.gov/ accounting-standards/authoritative-source-of-gaap/.

[5] Federal Accounting Standards Advisory Board, "SFFAC 1," p. 21.

[6] Federal Accounting Standards Advisory Board, "SFFAC 2," in *FASAB Handbook of Federal Accounting Standards and Other Pronouncements, as Amended*, p. 5. FASAB does not, however, identify those entities actually responsible for preparing and issuing financial statements. Federal statutes, as explained below, enumerate which agencies must issue federal financial reports.

[7] Federal Accounting Standards Advisory Board, "SFFAC 1," p. 1.

[8] Ibid., p. 2.

[9] Federal Accounting Standards Advisory Board, "SFFAC 2," p. 22.

[10] Office of Management and Budget, *Financial Reporting Requirements*, August 3, 2012, at http://www.whitehouse.gov/sites/default/files/omb/assets

[11] Federal Accounting Standards Advisory Board, "SFFAC 1," p. 46.

[12] U.S. Department of the Treasury, *2011 Financial Report of the United States Government*, at http://www.fms.treas.gov/frsummary/frsummary2011.pdf.

[13] Federal Accounting Standards Advisory Board, "SFFAC 1," p. 37.

[14] Ibid.

[15] Office of Management and Budget, Circular A-123, *Management's Responsibility for Internal Control*, December 21, 2004, at http://www.whitehouse.gov/sites/default/files/omb/ assets/omb/circulars/a123/a123_rev.pdf.

[16] "SFFAC 1," p. 23.

[17] Joseph Story, *Commentaries on the Constitution* (Boston: Hilliard, Gray, and Company, 1833), vol. 3, §§ 1341-43, at http://press-pubs.uchicago.edu/founders/documents/a1_9_7s4.html.

[18] Senator Tom Coburn, "Amendment #3111, Importance of Audit the Pentagon Act–Talking Points," undated, at http://www.coburn.senate.gov/public//index.cfm?a=Files. Serve&File_id=eb595449-4af1-4c8c-a6d3-f1567b1fc60c

[19] U.S. Congress, House of Representatives, *Annals of Congress*, 2nd Cong., 1st sess., December 30, 1791, p. 302.

[20] 28 Stat. 205, July 31, 1894 (at 210). The Dockery Act, it has been written, provided "for a greater centralization of accounting functions and for a single audit of accounts in place of the ancient and cumbersome system of triplicate audits." Paul Studenski and Herman E. Kroos, *Financial History of the United States* (New York: McGraw-Hill Book Company, 1952), p. 224.

[21] 34 Stat. 949, February 26, 1907.

[22] 64 Stat. 832, September 12, 1950.

[23] 64 Stat. 835.

[24] 64 Stat. 836.

[25] Ibid.

[26] 104 Stat. 2838, November 15, 1990.

[27] General Accounting Office, *The Chief Financial Officers Act: A Mandate for Federal Financial Management Reform*, GAO/AFMD-12.19.4, September 1991, p. 1, at http://www.gao.gov/special.pubs/af12194.pdf.

[28] The latter provision was expanded to every covered CFO agency under GMRA and to every executive agency under ATDA.

[29] For an assessment of the CFO Act, see the Chief Financial Officers Council and the Council of Inspectors General on Integrity and Efficiency, *The Chief Financial Officers Act of 1990—20 Years Later*, July 2011, at http://www.ignet.gov/ randp/cigiecforpt0711.pdf.

[30] 108 Stat. 3410, October 13, 1994.

[31] U.S. Congress, Senate, Committee on Governmental Affairs, *Government Management Reform Act of 1994*, report to accompany S. 2170, 2nd sess., S. Rept. 103rd Congress (Washington: GPO, 1994), p. 1. For example, the statute established a pilot program in 6 agencies that permitted them to sell ("franchise") services to other federal agencies, and also limited the automatic cost of living raises for Members of Congress, the Executive Schedule, and the judiciary to not exceed those given to General Schedule (GS) federal employees. The statute emerged subsequent to the National Performance Review of President William J. Clinton and Vice President Albert Gore, Jr. See Office of the Vice President, "From Red Tape to Results: Creating a Government that Works Better & Costs Less: Report of the National Performance Review," 1993.

[32] For a current list of CFO agencies, see the **Appendix**.

[33] 116 Stat. 2049, November 7, 2002.

[34] 116 Stat. 2049.

[35] U.S. Congress, Senate Committee on Governmental Affairs, Accountability of Tax Dollars Act of 2002, report to accompany S. 2644, 107th Congress, 2nd sess., S.Rept. 107-331 (Washington: GPO, 2002), p. 1.

[36] General Accounting Office, Financial Integrity Act: Inadequate Controls Result in Ineffective Federal Programs and Billions in Losses, GAO/AFMD-90-10, November 1989, p. 4, at http://www.gao.gov/assets

[37] General Accounting Office, Financial Management Reform, T-AFMD-90-31, September 17, 1990, p. 2, at http://www.gao.gov/assets

[38] General Accounting Office, Managing The Cost Of Government: Building An Effective Financial Management Structure, GAO/AFMD-85-35-A, February 1985, p. 11, at http://archive.gao.gov/d10t2/126342.pdf.

[39] Ibid.

[40] General Accounting Office, *The Chief Financial Officers Act: A Mandate for Federal Financial Management Reform*, p. 14.

[41] General Accounting Office, *Managing The Cost Of Government: Building An Effective Financial Management Structure*, pp. 13-14.

[42] Ibid.

[43] General Accounting Office, *Financial Integrity Act: Inadequate Controls Result in Ineffective Federal Programs and Billions in Losses*, p. 54.

[44] General Accounting Office, *Financial Management: CFO Act Is Achieving Meaningful Progress*, GAO/T-AIMD-94- 149, June 21, 1994, p. 1, at http://www.gao.gov/assets/110/105597.pdf.

[45] Chief Financial Officers Council and the Council of Inspectors General on Integrity and Efficiency, *The Chief Financial Officers Act of 1990—20 Years Later*, p. 13.

[46] As amended by GMRA and ATDA.

[47] Chief Financial Officers Council and the Council of Inspectors General on Integrity and Efficiency, *The Chief Financial Officers Act of 1990—20 Years Later*, p. 12.

[48] An unqualified or clean opinion means that an agency's financial statements are free of material misstatements and accord with Generally Accepted Accounting Principles (GAAP). Office of Management and Budget, *Audit Requirements for Federal Financial Statements*, OMB Bulletin No. 07-04, September 4, 2007, p. 14, at http://www.whitehouse.gov/sites/

default/files/omb/assets/omb/bulletins/fy2007/b07-04.pdf. There are three other types of audit opinions: a qualified opinion is issued when financial statements are fairly presented but there is a misstatement or some portion of the financial statements could not be audited; an adverse opinion states that the information contained in the financial statements is materially incorrect; and a disclaimer of opinion indicates that the auditor is unable to form an opinion on the financial statements.

[49] Chief Financial Officers Council and the Council of Inspectors General on Integrity and Efficiency, *The Chief Financial Officers Act of 1990—20 Years Later*, p. 13.

[50] The President's budget submission for FY2013 includes a request for $613.9 billion in discretionary budget authority for DOD. Office of the Under Secretary of Defense (Comptroller)/Chief Financial Officer, *Overview: United States Department of Defense Fiscal Year 2013 Budget Request*, February 2012, p. 1-1, at http://comptroller.defense.gov/defbudget/fy2013/FY2013_Budget_Request_Overview_Book.pdf. According to GAO, this represents about 57 percent of the discretionary federal budget authority requested for FY2013. Government Accountability Office, *DOD Financial Management: Challenges in Attaining Audit Readiness and Improving Business Processes and Systems*, GAO-12- 642T, pp. 2-3, at http://www.gao.gov/assets

[51] According to OMB, "A material weakness is defined as a significant deficiency, or combination of significant deficiencies, that result in a more than remote likelihood that a material misstatement of the financial statements will not be prevented or detected." Office of Management and Budget, *Audit Requirements for Federal Financial Statements*, p. 6.

[52] With regard to internal control over financial reporting, one or more material weaknesses would not necessarily affect the overall audit opinion, provided that the material weaknesses do not result in a limitation on the scope of the auditor's work.

[53] Government Accountability Office, *CFO Act of 1990: Driving the Transformation of Federal Financial Management*, GAO-06-242T, November 17, 2005, p. 16, at http://www.gao.gov/new.items/d06242t.pdf.

[54] U.S. Department of Labor, *Agency Financial Report: Fiscal Year 2011*, November 14, 2011, p. 35, at http://www.dol.gov/_sec/media

[55] DOL's Office of the Chief Financial Officer (OFCO) ultimately provided revised data to the auditors that permitted reconciliation. Ibid., p. 41.

[56] Office of Management and Budget, *Increase Reliability of Financial Information*, Performance.gov, at http://finance.performance.gov/initiative/increase-reliability

[57] Ibid.

[58] Government Accountability Office, *Financial Audit: U.S. Government's Fiscal Years 2012 and 2011 Consolidated Financial Statements*, GAO-13-271R, January 17, 2013, p. 28, at http://www.gao.gov/assets

[59] Office of Management and Budget, *Increase Reliability of Financial Information*, Performance.gov, at http://finance.performance.gov/initiative/increase-reliability

[60] U.S. Department of Homeland Security, *U.S. Department of Homeland Security Annual Financial Report: Fiscal Year 2011*, November 11, 2011, p. 256, at http://www.dhs.gov/xlibrary/assets

[61] U.S. Department of Homeland Security, *Annual Financial Report: Fiscal Year 2012*, November 15, 2012, p. 193, at http://www.dhs.gov/sites/default/files/publications/dhs-annual-financial

[62] Ibid., pp. 280-281.

[63] Ibid., p. 281. The DHS Audit Requirement Target Act of 2012 (DART, 126 Stat. 1591), which requires DHS to obtain an unqualified audit opinion beginning with its FY2013 annual financial statements, was passed soon after the publication of DHS's Annual Financial Report for FY2012. The DART Act will be discussed in a subsequent section of this chapter.

[64] Government Accountability Office, *DOD Financial Management: Improvement Needed in DOD Components' Implementation of Audit Readiness Effort*, GAO-11-851, September 2011, p. 4, at http://www.gao.gov/new.items/ d11851.pdf; Office of Management and

Budget, *Increase Reliability of Financial Information*, Performance.gov, at http://finance.performance.gov/initiative/increase-reliability

[65] U.S. Congress, House Committee on Oversight and Government Reform, Subcommittee on Government Organization, Efficiency, and Financial Management, *The Department of Defense: Challenges in Financial Management*, 112th Cong., 1st sess., September 23, 2011, H. Hrg. HRG-2011-CGR-0103, p. 23.

[66] Ibid., p. 25.

[67] Ibid.

[68] Ibid., p. 27.

[69] Ibid.

[70] The 13 auditor-identified material weaknesses are: Financial Management Systems; Fund Balance with Treasury; Accounts Receivable; Inventory; Operating Materials and Supplies; General Property, Plant, and Equipment; Government Property in Possession of Contractors; Accounts Payable; Environmental Liabilities; Statement of Net Cost; Intragovernmental Eliminations; Accounting Entries; and Reconciliation of Net Cost of Operations to Budget. U.S. Department of Defense, *Agency Financial Report: Fiscal Year 2012*, November 15, 2012, p. 73, at http://comptroller.defense.gov/afr/fy2012/DoD_FY12_Agency_Financial_Report.pdf.

[71] U.S. Congress, House Committee on Oversight and Government Reform, Subcommittee on Government Organization, Efficiency, and Financial Management, *The Department of Defense: Challenges in Financial Management*, p. 35.

[72] Ibid.

[73] Ibid., p. 38.

[74] Ibid.

[75] Ibid., p. 39.

[76] Government Accountability Office, *DOD Financial Management: Numerous Challenges Must Be Addressed to Improve Reliability of Financial Information*, GAO-11-835T, July 27, 2011, Highlights Page, http://www.gao.gov/ assets/130/126745.pdf. Financial management at DOD remains on GAO's high-risk list. Government Accountability Office, *High-Risk Series: An Update*, GAO-13-283, February 2013, pp. 134-141, at http://www.gao.gov/assets/660/ 652133.pdf.

[77] Statement of Senator Kelly Ayotte, U.S. Congress, Senate Committee on Armed Services, Subcommittee on Readiness and Management Support, *Financial Management and Business Transformation at the Department of Defense*, 112th Cong., 2nd sess., April 18, 2012, S. Hrg. 112–658, p. 3.

[78] House Armed Services Committee, *Panel on Defense Financial Management and Auditability Reform: Findings and Recommendations*, 112th Cong., 2nd sess., January 24, 2012.

[79] The U.S. government's accrual-based consolidated financial statements are contained in the annual *Financial Report of the United States Government.*

[80] Under GMRA, the first government-wide financial statement was required no later than March 31, 1998.

[81] Government Accountability Office, *Financial Audit: U.S. Government's Fiscal Years 2012 and 2011 Consolidated Financial Statements*, p. 224.

[82] Gene L. Dodaro, Comptroller General, Government Accountability Office, *Financial Audit: U.S. Government's Fiscal Years 2012 and 2011 Consolidated Financial Statements*, GAO-13-271R, January 17, 2013, Transmission Letter–2, at http://www.gao.gov/assets/660/651357.pdf.

[83] Ibid. See also Government Accountability Office, Fiscal Year 2011 U.S. Government Financial Statements: The Federal Government Faces Continuing Financial Management and Long-Term Fiscal Challenges, GAO-12-444T, March 1, 2012, p. 6, at http://www.gao.gov/assets/590/589002.pdf.

[84] Government Accountability Office, *Financial Audit: U.S. Government's Fiscal Years 2012 and 2011 Consolidated Financial Statements*, p. 227.

[85] Ibid.

[86] Ibid.

[87] See CRS Report R42878, *Improper Payments and Recovery Audits: Legislation, Implementation, and Analysis*, by Garrett Hatch.

[88] Government Accountability Office, *Financial Audit: U.S. Government's Fiscal Years 2012 and 2011 Consolidated Financial Statements*, pp. 243-246.

[89] Government Accountability Office, *Management Report: Improvements Needed in Controls over the Preparation of the U.S. Consolidated Financial Statements*, GAO-13-540, June 2013, p 10.

[90] Ibid.

[91] Chief Financial Officers Council and the Council of Inspectors General on Integrity and Efficiency, *The Chief Financial Officers Act of 1990—20 Years Later*, p. 16.

[92] FASAB, *Financial Reporting Model Task Force: Report to the FASAB*, December 22, 2010, p. 10, at http://www.fasab.gov/pdffiles/2010dec22_financial

[93] Ibid., p. 15.

[94] FASAB, *User Needs Study*, April 14, 2010.

[95] FASAB, *Financial Reporting Model Task Force: Report to the FASAB*, p. 11.

[96] KPMG Government Institute, *Moving to the Next Stage of Federal Financial Reporting: Bringing Greater Value and Transparency through "Open Government" Electronic Reporting*, July 6, 2012, p. 6, at http://www.kpmginstitutes.com/government-institute/insights/2012/pdf/federal-financial

[97] Statement of Representative Edolphus Towns, U.S. Congress, House Committee on Oversight and Government Reform, Subcommittee on Government Organization, Efficiency, and Financial Management, *Making Sense of the Numbers: Improving the Federal Financial Reporting Model*, 112th Cong., 1st sess., February 16, 2011, H. Hrg. HRG- 2011-CGR-0007, pp. 3-4.

[98] FASAB, *Financial Reporting Model Task Force: Report to the FASAB*, p. 11.

[99] General Accounting Office, *Financial Reporting: Framework for Analyzing Federal Agency Financial Statements*, GAO/AFMD-91-19, March 1991, pp. 11-12, at http://gao.justia.com/department-of-veterans-affairs/1991/3/financial- reporting-afmd-91-19/AFMD-91-19-full-report.pdf.

[100] 123 Stat. 2439-2441.

[101] S. 3487 defines "validated as ready for audit" to mean that DOD's audit agencies would have reviewed the financial statements and determined, in writing, that such statements are ready for audit.

[102] Milestone B is defined as a decision to enter into system development and demonstration pursuant to guidance prescribed by the Secretary of Defense for the management of Department of Defense acquisition programs (10 U.S.C. 2366(e)(7)).

[103] Representative Lee introduced the legislation on February 6, 2013.

[104] There are some differences between H.R. 6528 and H.R. 559. The summary of H.R. 559 includes the word "qualified" in reference to an agency's overall audit opinion, though the text of both H.R. 6528 and H.R. 559 in Sec. 4(c)(2) refers to unqualified and qualified audit opinions. Sec. 4(c)(1) of H.R. 6528 and H.R. 559 contains the financial accountability deadline (i.e., March 2 of each fiscal year in question is when the discretionary budgetary authority adjustment would be imposed). The initial fiscal year would have been FY2013 in H.R. 6528 but was changed to FY2014 in H.R. 559. Lastly, H.R. 559 eliminates the reporting requirement in Sec. 5(1) of H.R. 6528 that would have required the Under Secretary of Defense (Comptroller) to submit a report to Congress itemizing those reports that would no longer be necessary if the financial statements of the Department of Defense were audited with an unqualified opinion.

[105] U.S. Congress, Senate Committee on Homeland Security and Governmental Affairs, *DHS Audit Requirement Target (DART) Act of 2012*, report to accompany S. 1998, 112th Cong., 2nd sess., November 2, 2012, p. 1.

[106] 126 Stat. 339.

In: Federal Financial Reporting
Editor: Denise Mahoney
ISBN: 978-1-62948-871-4

Chapter 2

UNDERSTANDING THE PRIMARY COMPONENTS OF THE ANNUAL FINANCIAL REPORT OF THE UNITED STATES GOVERNMENT*

United States Government Accountability Office

THE CONSOLIDATED FINANCIAL REPORT

Similar to a corporation's annual report, the Consolidated Financial Report (CFR) is the federal government's general-purpose report of accountability to the American public on its finances. It is intended to

- provide an overall view of the annual financial results of operations and the financial position of the federal government, including long-term commitments and obligations;
- demonstrate accountability for the money the federal government raises through taxes and for spending money according to the laws and regulations that govern the federal government's budgets and financial operations;

* This is an edited, reformatted and augmented version of the United States Government Accountability Office Report, GAO-09-946SP dated September 2009.

- report on the federal government's operating performance, accounting systems, and internal control; and
- demonstrate the federal government's stewardship over its resources.

The consolidated financial statements (CFS) in the CFR, submitted by the Department of the Treasury in coordination with the Office of Management and Budget, present consolidated and summarized financial information from the various federal government agencies and departments. The federal government is responsible for

- preparing the annual CFS in conformity with U.S. generally accepted accounting principles;
- establishing, maintaining, and assessing internal control to provide reasonable assurance that the control objectives of the Federal Managers' Financial Integrity Act, 31 U.S.C. 3512 (c), (d) are met; and
- complying with applicable laws and regulations.

The Federal Accounting Standards Advisory Board (FASAB), after considering the financial and budgetary information needs of citizens, congressional oversight groups, executive agencies, and other users, promulgates the accounting and reporting standards essential for public accountability over federal dollars.

GAO conducts the audit of the CFS, along with the accompanying notes to the financial statements; the objective is to provide an opinion on the fairness of the consolidated financial statements taken as a whole.

The CFR Is Organized into Seven Major Sections

A Citizen's Guide	Management's Discussion and Analysis	Financial Statements	Notes to the Financial Statements	Supplemental Information	Stewardship Information	Government Accountability Office Report

- **A Citizen's Guide** highlights significant information found in the CFR.
- **Management's Discussion and Analysis** provides management's insights into the information presented in the federal government's financial statements.

- **Financial Statements** consolidate financial information from federal entities to provide an overall view of the federal government's financial operations and condition.
- **Notes to the Financial Statements** provide important disclosures and details related to information reported on the financial statements.
- **Supplemental Information** provides additional information to enhance the understanding of the federal government's operations and financial condition.
- **Stewardship Information** highlights substantial investments that have long-term benefits to the public including programs related to nonfederal physical property, human capital, and research and development.
- **Government Accountability Office** Report presents the results of GAO's audit of the financial statements and notes to the financial statements.

This guide discusses the significant content of each section in the CFR, with a primary emphasis on the federal government's financial statements.

A CITIZEN'S GUIDE

The purpose of the Citizen's Guide is to provide a high-level overview of significant information found in the CFR. The fiscal year 2008 guide includes information on the following:

- Significant increases in the net operating cost and the unified budget deficit from fiscal year 2007 to fiscal year 2008. The net operating cost for the government's annual operations— the difference between revenue and net cost—increased from $276 billion for fiscal year 2007 to just over $1 trillion for fiscal year 2008. Total federal government revenue remained relatively constant compared to fiscal year 2007. However, the federal government's net cost increased by $731 billion, or more than 25 percent, over fiscal year 2007. Approximately half of this increase was related to net cost increases at the Department of Veterans Affairs, primarily those related to increases in estimated actuarial liabilities for veterans' benefits. The unified budget deficit (primarily cash basis) for the year more than doubled, from $163 billion in fiscal year 2007 to $455 billion in fiscal year 2008, due in part to the weakening economy in fiscal year 2008.

- U.S. government actions to address the housing and credit market crisis and the economic recession. The Housing and Economic Recovery Act and the Emergency Economic Stabilization Act of 2008 were enacted in an effort to stabilize the financial sector and protect the economy. Actions taken in response to these legislative initiatives have the potential to significantly increase future borrowing by the government, and their impact will largely be reflected in the financial statements for fiscal year 2009 and beyond.
- The unsustainability of the federal government's existing fiscal policies. Under current policy, Medicare and Medicaid spending driven by escalating growth in health care costs and an aging population, along with scheduled higher Social Security spending due to an aging population, will significantly increase overall federal spending. Total government expenditures are projected to exceed federal revenues each year, resulting in permanent annual deficits that grow larger and larger. As the deficits grow, so does the need for more borrowing from the public. Projections under current policy show government debt levels reaching unprecedented and unsustainable levels.

Management Discussion and Analysis

The Management's Discussion and Analysis (MD&A) section of the CFR provides important insights into the information presented in the federal government's financial statements. It presents management's perspective on the financial information and overall operations of the federal government in more detail than the Citizen's Guide.

The MD&A is intended to provide readers with a narrative overview and analysis of the federal government's performance, financial position, and financial operations. It is also intended to address the federal government's financial statements, systems and controls, compliance with laws and regulations, and actions taken or planned to address problems. For example, the fiscal year 2008 MD&A

- discusses the economic recession of the United States as a backdrop to the financial condition of the federal government for fiscal year 2008.

It includes a summary of some key economic indicators, such as the ongoing slump in the residential homebuilding sector, record high energy prices, elevated food prices, increasing job losses, and the weakening or declining of corporate profits outside the energy sector.

- explains the volatility of the housing and credit markets during the last half of fiscal year 2008, which sparked unprecedented economic events. Major problems in the subprime credit market led the way for significant losses in mortgage backed securities and substantial cash shortfalls for the investment banks, government sponsored enterprises involved in the secondary housing financial market, and bank investors. This precarious environment has resulted in the transformation, acquisition, and even the demise of several leading and long-established major financial institutions. Also, the MD&A discusses the federal government's intended actions to provide stability in the housing and credit markets.
- discusses important fiscal issues and significant conditions that affect the country's future fiscal health. Emphasis is given to the estimated cost and exposures under current policy to pay benefits of key social insurance programs such as Social Security and Medicare. It provides historical data as well as forward looking projections of how the aging of the population and continually rising health care costs could lead to further erosion of the federal government's fiscal health.
- graphically depicts important information, such as the federal government's revenues and costs, or "what came in and what went out," over the past several years, and the federal government's increasing liabilities, or "what we owe," by major components.

Financial Statements

Some Important Financial Statement Concepts

Before considering the purpose and content of each of the federal government's consolidated financial statements, it is important to understand certain concepts about the nature of those financial statements, especially the (1) use of cash and accrual accounting and (2) treatment of transactions between federal entities.

Cash and Accrual Accounting

Except for the Statement of Social Insurance, the federal government generally uses both the accrual basis and cash basis of accounting to record and report financial information. Accrual accounting, also used in the private sector, is generally the basis used to prepare the Statement of Net Cost, Statement of Operations and Changes in Net Position, and the Balance Sheet. It is intended to provide a complete picture of the federal government's financial operations and financial position. In contrast, the federal government primarily uses the cash basis of accounting for its budget, which is the federal government's primary financial planning and control tool. The budget helps establish national spending priorities and helps ensure that the federal government spends taxpayers' money in accordance with applicable appropriations laws. Information on the most recent President's Budget can be found on the Office of Management and Budget's website at http://www.whitehouse.gov/omb/ budget. Differences between the federal government's operating results and its budget results are shown in the statement called the Reconciliation of Net Operating Revenue (or Cost) and Unified Budget Surplus (or Deficit). Accordingly, understanding the basic concepts of the cash basis and accrual basis of accounting is important to understanding the information included in the federal government's financial statements.

Cash Basis of Accounting

Because it is similar to keeping a checkbook, the cash basis of accounting (used to account for and report budget results) is perhaps the easier of the two bases of accounting to understand. The cash basis focus is on cash receipts, cash disbursements, and the difference between the two amounts. With relatively few exceptions, receipts are recorded when cash is received, and outlays are recorded when cash is disbursed. The difference between cash receipts and cash outlays at the end of the fiscal year is reported as the annual budget surplus or budget deficit. For example, for fiscal year 2008 the federal government reported a unified budget deficit of about $455 billion (explained in more detail later in this guide). This deficit was based on reported cash outlays of about $2,979 billion compared with reported cash receipts of about $2,524 billion. It is important to note that the federal government's cash receipts used in determining the unified budget deficit include surplus funds earmarked for the Social Security trust funds and certain other trust funds.

Accrual Basis of Accounting

The accrual basis of accounting recognizes revenue when it is earned and recognizes expenses in the period incurred, without regard to when cash is received or disbursed. The federal government, which receives most of its revenue from taxes, nevertheless, recognizes tax revenue when it is collected, under an accepted modified cash basis of accounting.

Expenses are recognized during the period in which they are incurred. Accrual accounting, for example, recognizes that while the employee is working, the employee earns not only a salary but also health, pension, and other benefits that will be paid in the future during the employee's retirement. Accordingly, each year, on the basis of actuarial calculations of benefits earned, the federal government records as an expense (operating cost) an estimated amount for these earned benefits and increases the related liability—Federal Employee and Veteran Benefits Payable—for the amount owed to its employees, both civilian and military. Thus, the accrual basis of accounting is intended to provide a complete financial picture, for the CFR reader, of the federal government's annual employee-related costs.

Also under accrual accounting, the federal government reports physical assets when they are acquired and records related expenses when the federal government benefits from their use or consumption or when they are sold. Physical assets consist of inventories of goods held for sale or for future consumption and long-lived or "fixed" assets such as land, buildings, and equipment. In the case of assets such as buildings and equipment, the annual cost attributed to their use is recorded as depreciation expense.

Treatment of Transactions between Federal Entities

In the normal course of federal government operations, federal agencies and departments frequently purchase and sell goods and services among themselves. These types of activities between federal agencies and departments are called intragovernmental transactions. They also include amounts the federal government borrows from the Social Security trust funds. Intragovernmental transactions are recorded in federal agencies' and departments' accounts and financial statements along with transactions conducted with nonfederal entities. These intragovernmental transactions are to be eliminated from the federal government's consolidated accounts and financial statements so that the totals for the affected accounts, when summarized for all federal government agencies and departments, are not overstated for the federal government as a whole.

Composition of the Financial Statements

The federal government's consolidated financial statements include six statements (pages 31 and 32 of this guide provide discussion and a simplified overview of how the five accrual-basis financial statements are related). The first five financial statements below (accrual-basis financial statements) present 2 years of financial data so that readers can compare the federal government's financial information for the current and prior years. The sequence in which the financial statements appear below are the order in which they appear in the CFR.

Statement of Net Cost	Statement of Operations and Changes in Net Position	Reconciliation of Net Operating Revenue (or Cost) and Unified Budget Surplus (or Deficit)	Statement of Changes in Cash Balance from Unified Budget and Other Activities	Balance Sheet	Statement of Social Insurance

- **Statement of Net Cost -** The first statement shows the annual costs on the accrual basis of accounting, to operate the federal government in total, and by major department and agency.
- **Statement of Operations and Changes in Net Position** - The second statement shows the accrual-based results of the federal government's operations—the extent to which the federal government's tax revenue covers its net cost. It also shows how these annual results (called the net operating revenue or net operating cost) affect the federal government's net financial position as of a given date—the difference between its assets (what it owns) and its liabilities (what it owes).
- **Reconciliation of Net Operating Revenue (or Cost) and Unified Budget Surplus (or Deficit)** - The third statement shows the relationship between the accrual-based operating results and the cash-based budget results. It begins with the net operating result (revenue or cost) from the Statement of Operations and Changes in Net Position and shows the items that explain the difference between that amount and the federal government's annual cash-based budget surplus or deficit.

- **Statement of Changes in Cash Balance from Unified Budget and Other Activities -** The fourth statement shows the relationship between the cash-based budget surplus or deficit and the change in the balance of cash and other monetary assets. It begins with the cash-based budget surplus or deficit and shows the items that explain either how the federal government used a budget surplus or financed a budget deficit.
- **Balance Sheet -** The fifth statement shows the nature and amount of the federal government's assets (what it owns) and liabilities (what it owes) and the difference between the two, called the net position. This net position amount is the same as the net position amount reported in the Statement of Operations and Changes in Net Position.
- **Statement of Social Insurance -** The sixth financial statement shows how much money in addition to earmarked revenue the federal government estimates it would need today, under current policy, to cover the projected long-term commitments of its major social insurance programs, such as Social Security and Medicare. Beginning in fiscal year 2006, the Statement of Social Insurance became a basic financial statement, with the key economic and demographic assumptions disclosed in the accompanying notes to the CFS, and with other social insurance related information presented in the Supplemental Information section of the CFR. Prior to fiscal year 2006, all social insurance related information was presented as Stewardship Information in the CFR.

The amount of revenue directed to earmarked funds, such as the Social Security trust funds, has increased dramatically over the past 2 decades and now constitutes a greater proportion of the federal budget. To improve the transparency of this important source of revenue, FASAB issued a standard for identifying and reporting earmarked funds. According to FASAB, an earmarked fund receives specifically identified revenue and other financing sources that (1) remain available over time, (2) are required by statute to be used for designated activities, benefits, or purposes, and (3) must be accounted for separately from the government's general revenues. Beginning in the fiscal year 2006 CFR, earmarked revenue is shown separately on the Statement of Operations and Changes in Net Position. In addition, the Balance Sheet shows separately the portion of net position attributable to earmarked funds. Additional financial information regarding the major earmarked funds is provided in the notes to the financial statements under the caption Earmarked

Funds. This information is intended to assist users of financial statements in understanding the federal government's results of operations and related commitments.

Beginning in fiscal year 2009, the CFR will include additional information on fiduciary activities, such as the Federal Employees' Thrift Savings Fund. Fiduciary activities relate to the collection or receipt and the subsequent management, protection, accounting, investment, and disposition of cash or other assets in which nonfederal individuals or entities have an ownership interest that the federal government must uphold. Fiduciary assets are not assets of the federal government and therefore, will not be recognized on the Balance Sheet of the U.S. government.

The following sections discuss each of these six statements in additional detail and offer insights regarding potential uses and analytical data available from each.

STATEMENT OF NET COST

The Statement of Net Cost is intended to show how much it cost to operate the federal government, by federal agency and department, and in total. It provides costs on an accrual basis of accounting, which recognizes expenses when they are incurred, regardless of when cash is disbursed. Thus, it provides, for the accounting period, cost information that can be related to the goods produced, services rendered, and the outcomes of the programs of the federal government's agencies and departments for the same period. Since the actuarial calculations for social insurance costs are not reported as liabilities on the Balance Sheet, the corresponding costs also are excluded from the cost of government operations. An important concept of the Statement of Net Cost is that the revenue earned by federal agencies and departments from their operations, such as admissions to national parks and fees paid for postal services and stamps, is subtracted from their cost of operations. The net cost is the amount to be financed from tax revenue and, as needed, borrowing.

Readers can use this statement to find such information as

- which agencies or departments accounted for most of the federal government's net cost,

- how much the federal government's net cost increased or decreased from the prior fiscal year, and
- which agency or department experienced the largest increase and which experienced the largest decrease in net cost from the previous year.

Illustrative Net Cost Information

(In billions of dollars)	Year ended Sept. 30 2008			Year ended Sept. 30 2007		
	● Gross Cost	■ Earned Revenue	▲ Net Cost	Gross Cost	Earned Revenue	Net Cost
Department of Defense	767.6	26.8	740.8	689.6	25.1	664.5
Department of Health and Human Services	769.1	56.4	712.7	718.6	51.8	666.8
Social Security Administration	663.9	.3	663.6	626.4	.3	626.1
Department of Veterans Affairs	434.6	4.2	430.4	63.1	3.7	59.4
Interest on Treasury securities held by the public	241.6	—	241.6	238.9	—	238.9
Department of Energy	35.8	4.2	31.6	67.5	4.3	63.2
All other entities	979.0	159.0	820.0	753.2	162.6	590.6
Total	**3,891.6**	**250.9**	**3,640.7**	**3,157.3**	**247.8**	**2,909.5**

● **Gross Cost** is the accrual-based total cost of the federal government's operations for the year. The statement presents gross cost, earned revenue, and net cost by federal agency and department. Also, it includes the cost of interest on Treasury securities held by the public, which includes foreign investors.

■ **Earned Revenue** comes from fees charged for goods and services. The fees charged for postal services such as stamps are a well-known example of earned revenue. Earned revenue shows how much the federal agencies and departments earn from their operations to cover their gross costs, as opposed to relying on taxes and borrowing to cover the costs.

▲ **Net Cost** is the portion of the gross cost left after subtracting earned revenue. The federal government funds the net cost of government from tax revenue and, as needed, by borrowing.

Over half of the federal government's fiscal year 2008 net costs came from three agencies or departments: the Department of Defense, the Department of Health and Human Services, and the Social Security Administration. Together, these three accounted for about $2.1 trillion, or 58 percent of the approximately $3.6 trillion of reported total net costs. The reported 2008 total net cost was substantially more than in 2007 by, $731.2 billion or about 25 percent. The largest cost increase, by agency or department, was $371 billion for the Department of Veterans Affairs, mostly related to increases in veterans-benefit actuarial liabilities for compensation benefits to veterans who are disabled by military service–related causes. The Department of Energy reported the largest cost decrease of $31.6 billion, primarily due to changes in environmental cleanup and disposal liability estimates. It is important to note that agencies or departments that use actuarial projections in determining their costs and related liabilities may experience large fluctuations in annual costs due to program benefit changes and changes to actuarial assumptions.

STATEMENT OF OPERATIONS AND CHANGES IN NET POSITION

Similar to corporations' income statements, the Statement of Operations and Changes in Net Position shows the annual financial results of federal operations (tax revenue less net cost) and how these results affect net position—the difference between its assets and liabilities.

The Statement of Operations and Changes in Net Position shows activity for earmarked and nonearmarked funds. Earmarked funds are financed by specific revenue that remain available over time for designated purposes. For example, the Federal Old-Age and Survivors Insurance and Federal Disability Insurance programs, collectively referred to as "Social Security," are financed through payroll and self-employment taxes. These programs provide a basic income supplement to retired workers; to survivors, in the event of death of a family's primary wage earner; and for protection against the loss of earnings due to a wage earner's disability. Other major earmarked funds include the Medicare trust funds, Military Retirement Fund, and Civil Service Retirement and Disability fund. The financial condition and operating results of each of these major funds can be found in the CFS' disclosure note, Earmarked Funds.

Nonearmarked funds are financed by nonearmarked receipts and proceeds of general borrowing. These funds finance the remaining federal government activities, and often are designated to supplement earmarked funds through appropriations and transfers, called intragovernmental transfers, on the Statement of Operations and Changes in Net Position. For example, Congress appropriated $180 billion in fiscal year 2008 to finance the Federal Supplementary Medical Insurance Trust Fund (Medicare Parts B and D).

Treasury borrows cash surpluses from certain earmarked funds (e.g., the Social Security trust funds) to help finance federal government operations, and it issues to the funds Treasury securities for the amounts borrowed. As of September 30, 2008, the reported investments in Treasury securities held by earmarked funds totaled about $4.2 trillion. Treasury pays interest on money borrowed from the earmarked funds. Both the related interest expense incurred by Treasury and the revenue earned by the earmarked funds, which totaled about $201 billion for fiscal year 2008, are shown on this statement and referred to as "intragovernmental interest." Such intragovernmental transactions are eliminated to avoid overstating the consolidated totals.

An important concept for this statement is the relationship between the results of operations and the changes in net position on the Balance Sheet. The annual financial results of federal operations should be directly reflected in the values of assets and liabilities, which determine the net financial position. For example, a net operating cost of $500 billion reduces the net position by $500 billion. However, unexplained differences between the net operating cost and the changes in net position have been reported in the Statement of Operations and Changes in Net Position as "Unmatched transactions and balances" as shown in the Illustrative Information on Operations and Changes in Net Position on the next page.

Readers can use this statement to find such information as

- the annual net operating cost or revenue for earmarked funds, nonearmarked funds, and the consolidated totals,
- how much tax revenue the federal government generated for the earmarked funds and nonearmarked funds for the fiscal year,
- how much nonearmarked funds were used to supplement earmarked funds, and
- whether the financial status of the federal government—its net position—has improved or deteriorated from the prior year.

Illustrative Information on Operations and Changes in Net Position

	(In billions of dollars)	Year ended Sept. 30, 2008		
	(Operations)	✱ Nonearmarked funds	✤ Earmarked funds	Consolidated totals
	Revenue:			
	Individual income tax and tax withholdings	1,210.0	868.4	2,078.4
	Corporate income and other taxes and miscellaneous revenues	451.7	131.3	583.0
✣	Intragovernmental interest	—	201.0	201.0
	Total Revenue	1,661.7	1,200.7	2,862.4
	Eliminations			(201.0)
▲	Consolidated Revenue			2,661.4
	Net Cost:			
	Net Cost	2,186.4	1,454.3	3,640.7
✣	Intragovernmental interest	201.0	—	201.0
	Total net cost	2,387.4	1,454.3	3,841.7
	Eliminations			(201.0)
◗	Consolidated net cost			3,640.7
♦	**Intragovernmental transfers**	(338.0)	338.0	—
●	**Unmatched transactions and balances**	(29.8)	—	(29.8))
∗	**Net Operating (Cost) Revenue**	(1,093.5)	84.4	(1,009.1
	(Changes in Net Position)			
❐	**Net Position, Beginning of Period**	(9,826.0)	620.2	(9,205.8)
	Adjustments to beginning balances	11.4	—	11.4
	Net Operating (Cost) Revenue	(1,093.5)	84.4	(1,009.1)
❐	**Net Position, End of Period**	(10,908.1)	704.6	(10,203.5)

✱ **Nonearmarked Funds** are financed by nonearmarked receipts and proceeds of general borrowing. These funds finance federal government activities that are not financed by earmarked funds.

✤ **Earmarked Funds** are financed by specific revenue that remains available over time for designated purposes. Major earmarked funds relate to Social Security and

Medicare programs, and military and civil service retirements and disability benefits.

✣ **Intragovernmental Interest** is the interest earned by earmarked funds and the interest paid by nonearmarked funds for money borrowed by the nonearmarked funds from the earmarked funds.

▲ **Consolidated Revenue** primarily comes from federal income tax collections, which includes taxes earmarked for Social Security and Medicare.

◗ **Consolidated Net Cost** is the net cost from the Statement of Net Cost.

♦ **Intragovernmental Transfers** supplement earmarked-fund activities, generally through appropriations from the Treasury General Fund.

● **Unmatched Transactions and Balances** are the unexplained differences between the Net Operating Cost and the Changes in Net Position.

∗ **Consolidated Net Operating (Cost) Revenue** is the financial results of operations—the difference between the revenue and the net cost of government operations for the fiscal year (plus or minus) the net amount of any unmatched transactions and balances.

❒ **Net Position** is the difference between the assets and liabilities reported on the Balance Sheet.

For example, the reported fiscal year 2008 consolidated net cost exceeded revenue by about $1 trillion, with nonearmarked funds reporting net operating cost of $1,093.5 billion and earmarked funds reporting a net operating surplus of $84.4 billion. For earmarked funds and nonearmarked funds, total reported revenues generated were about $1.2 trillion and $1.7 trillion, respectively. Also, the net cost of activities financed by the earmarked funds and nonearmarked funds were about $1.5 trillion and $2.4 trillion, respectively. Nonearmarked funds provided additional appropriations and transfers of $338 billion to earmarked funds.

Reconciliation of Net Operating Revenue (or Cost) and Unified Budget Surplus (or Deficit)

This statement is intended to demonstrate the federal government's accountability to the budget by reconciling its net operating cost to its unified budget results. The term "unified budget" refers to the budget compilation that includes the full range of federal activities, both "on-budget" and "off- budget" amounts. By law, Social Security and the Postal Service's activities are the only two material activities considered off-budget. On-budget programs and costs are those not excluded from the budget by law. The approximately $454.8 billion fiscal year 2008 unified budget deficit shown on the statement consists of about $638.1 billion on-budget deficit and approximately $183.3 billion off-budget surplus. The off-budget surplus for fiscal year 2008 consisted of $185.7 billion in surplus revenue from the Social Security trust funds offset by a $2.4 billion deficit in the Postal Service.

Readers can use this statement to find such information as

- major differences between the net operating cost and unified budget deficit,
- how much of the federal government's operating cost was attributable to the depreciation of its assets, and
- how much the federal government spent on capitalized fixed assets.

Illustrative Reconciliation of Net Operating Cost and Unified Budget Deficit

	(In billions of dollars)	Years ended Sept. 30	
		2008	**2007**
●	**Net Operating Cost** (Results of Operations)	(1,009.1)	(275.5)
■	**Components of Net Operating Cost Not Part of the Budget Deficit**		
	Increase in liabilities for employee and veteran benefits	549.8	90.1
	Increase in environmental and disposal liabilities	0.8	36.8
	Depreciation expense	54.8	45.3
	Other	70.4	25.0
▲	**Components of the Budget Deficit Not Part of the Net Operating Cost**		
	Cash outlays for capitalized fixed assets	(106.4)	(58.8)
	Other	(15.1)	(25.7)
✱	**The Unified Budget Deficit**	(454.8)	(162.8)

● **The Net Operating Cost** comes from the Statement of Operations and Changes in Net Position. It primarily represents the difference between the federal government's tax revenue and expenses.

■ **Components of Net Operating Cost Not Part of the Budget Deficit** are mostly current- year expenses under accrual accounting that do not involve current-year cash outlays. Increases in liabilities such as employee and veteran benefits and depreciation expense are recognized as current-year operating expenses under accrual accounting, but are not in the unified budget total.

▲ **Components of the Budget Deficit Not Part of Net Operating Cost** consist mostly of current- year cash outlays for transactions that do not involve current-year expenses, such as outlays to purchase buildings and equipment that the federal government capitalizes (records on its Balance Sheet as assets) and depreciates (expenses) as they are used in operations. The outlays to purchase these assets increase the unified budget deficit but not the current net operating cost.

✽ **The Unified Budget Deficit** represents the difference between cash receipts (primarily from taxes) and cash outlays for the year for all programs, on- and off-budget.

A major difference between the two bases of accounting for fiscal year 2008 is that changes in accrued expenses related to employee and veteran benefits, which totaled about $549.8 billion, are included in the net operating cost but not in the budget. In this statement, accrued benefit expenses are shown as an increase in liabilities for employee and veteran benefits. Also, the federal government reported about $54.8 billion for depreciation expense for fiscal year 2008, which is included in the net operating cost but not in the budget. In addition, the amount identified on this statement for the purchase of capitalized fixed assets for fiscal year 2008 totaled about $106.4 billion, consisting of approximately $71.6 billion for the Department of Defense and about $34.8 billion for all other federal agencies.

STATEMENT OF CHANGES IN CASH BALANCE FROM UNIFIED BUDGET AND OTHER ACTIVITIES

Since the federal government operates its budget principally on a cash basis, the primary purpose of the Statement of Changes in Cash Balance from Unified Budget and Other Activities is to report how the annual unified budget surplus or deficit relates to the federal government's borrowing (debt held by the public) and changes in the balance of cash and other monetary assets. It explains why a unified budget surplus or deficit normally would not result in an equal change in the balance of cash and other monetary assets.

Readers can use this statement to identify

- increases in federal borrowing as a result of the federal government's spending more than it collected in taxes,
- decreases in federal borrowing as a result of a budget surplus,
- changes in the balance of cash and other monetary assets, and
- how much cash the federal government spent to pay interest on debt held by the public.

Illustrative Information on Changes in Cash Balance from Unified Budget and Other Activities

	(In billions of dollars)	Years ended Sept. 30			
			2008		2007
	Unified Budget Deficit		(454.8)		(162.8)
	Adjustments for Noncash Outlays Included in the Budget				
■	Interest accrued by Treasury on debt held by the public	209.0		189.4	
	Subsidy expense	(3.0)		(9.3)	
	Subtotal		206.0		180.1
	Items Affecting the Cash Balance Not Included in the Budget				
	Net transactions from financing activity				
▲	Borrowings from the public	5,615.8		4,547.3	
▲	Repayment of debt held by the public	(4,853.1)		(4,340.4)	
	Other			(0.4)	
	Subtotal		762.7		206.5
	Net transactions from monetary and other activity				
■	Interest paid by Treasury on debt held by the public	(213.3)		(186.1)	
	Other	(4.1)		(7.6)	
	Subtotal		(217.4)		(193.7)
	Increase in Cash and Other Monetary Assets		296.5		30.1
	Cash and Other Monetary Assets Balance, Beginning of Period		128.0		97.9
	Cash and Other Monetary Assets Balance, End of Period		424.5		128.0

■ An exception to the primarily cash-based budget is the reporting of accrued interest on debt held by the public. To calculate the change in the balance of cash and other monetary assets, interest for the unified budget results is adjusted to include only the cash outlays. Specifically, the amount reported for **interest accrued by Treasury on debt held by the public** is added to the unified budget results and the amount reported **for interest paid by Treasury on debt held by the public** is subtracted from the unified budget results.

▲ The major financing activities include **borrowings from the public** and **repayment of debt held** by the public. Net borrowings provide operating cash needed to finance the budget deficit.

For example, for fiscal year 2008, the federal government reported that it increased its net borrowings from the public by about $762.7 billion to help finance the approximately $454.8 billion fiscal year 2008 unified budget deficit. It did this by borrowing about $5,615.8 billion from the public and paying off debts of approximately $4,853.1 billion. The federal government also reported that it used about $213.3 billion of its cash to pay interest on debt held by the public.

BALANCE SHEET

The Balance Sheet shows an end-of-year view of the federal government's overall financial position, its assets (what it owns), its liabilities (what it owes), and the difference between the two (its net position). It is important to note that the Balance Sheet does not include the value of the sovereign powers of the federal government to tax, regulate commerce, and set monetary policy. In addition, the federal government's responsibilities are much broader than the liabilities reported on the Balance Sheet, including the potential commitments related to and the impact of social insurance programs, such as Social Security and Medicare, over the long term. These resources and responsibilities are described in the Statement of Social Insurance, Notes to the Financial Statements, and the Supplemental Information section of the CFR.

Readers can use this statement to find such information as

- the makeup of the federal government's assets and liabilities,
- which liabilities increased the most, and
- whether the federal government has a positive net position—more assets than liabilities—or a negative net position—more liabilities than assets.

For example, the two largest liabilities as of the end of fiscal year 2008 are (1) about $5.8 trillion of debt held by the public, from whom the federal government borrowed money to pay for past deficits, and (2) about $5.3 trillion of pension and benefits owed to civilian employees and military personnel. These two items also account for the largest increases in liabilities for fiscal year 2008: federal debt held by the public and accrued interest increased by about $758.5 billion, and federal employee and veteran benefits payable increased by approximately $549.8 billion. As of the end of fiscal year 2008, the federal government's negative net position was about $10.2 trillion.

Illustrative Balance Sheet Information

(In billions of dollars)		As of Sept. 30	
		2008	2007 (Restated)
■	**Assets**		
	Cash and other monetary assets	424.5	128.0
	Loans receivable, net	263.4	231.9
	Inventories and related property, net	289.6	277.1
	Property, plant, and equipment, net	737.7	691.1
	Other assets	259.5	253.0
	Total assets	1,974.7	1,581.1
❋	**Stewardship Land and Heritage Assets**		
▲	**Liabilities**		
	Federal debt securities held by the public and accrued interest	5,836.2	5,077.7
	Federal employee and veteran benefits payable	5,318.9	4,769.1
	Environmental and disposal liabilities	342.8	342.0
	Other liabilities	680.3	598.1
	Total liabilities	12,178.2	10,786.9
●	**Commitments and Contingencies**		
♦	**Net Position**		
	Earmarked funds	704.6	620.2
	Nonearmarked funds	(10,908.1)	(9,826.0)
	Total net position	(10,203.5)	(9,205.8)
	Total liabilities and net position	1,974.7	1,581.1

- ■ **Assets** are the operational resources the federal government has available as of the end of the fiscal year. The largest category—property, plant, and equipment, net—

includes land and buildings and the federal government's military equipment, such as ships, aircraft, and tanks, after subtracting accumulated depreciation.

- ✻ **Stewardship Land and Heritage Assets**, which include national parks and natural resources, are reported in nonfinancial units in the notes to the financial statements.
- ▲ **Liabilities** are the financial responsibilities of the federal government as of the end of the fiscal year. In addition to federal debt securities, liabilities include federal employee and veteran benefits payable—the amount the federal government estimates that it owes or will owe its military and civilian employees and veterans under its life and health insurance and pension plans.
- ● Not all **Commitments and Contingencies** of the federal government require recognition as liabilities on the Balance Sheet. Commitments that require the future use of resources, such as long- term leases, as well as loss contingencies that are assessed to be at least reasonably possible, are disclosed in the notes to the financial statements.
- ♦ **Net Position** is the difference between the federal government's assets and liabilities.

Other Considerations

Certain federal trust funds, such as the Social Security trust funds, have been running cash surpluses, which are loaned to the Treasury and reduce the current need for the federal government to borrow from the public to finance current operations of the rest of the government. The transactions related to the use of such surpluses are eliminated from the federal government's Balance Sheet because, in effect, they represent loans from one part of the government to another. Importantly, these intragovernmental debt holdings, which are not shown on the Balance Sheet, constitute future obligations of the Treasury because the Treasury must provide cash to redeem these securities in order for the trust funds to pay benefits or other obligations as they come due.

Statement of Social Insurance

The Statement of Social Insurance shows how much more money would be needed, in today's dollars, for the federal government's social insurance programs to continue operating over the long term, as they are structured today. The estimates presented in these statements are based on actuarial projections of persons who are or will be participants in these programs. These estimates exclude related trust fund balances, primarily the special U.S. Treasury securities held by such trust funds. These securities are guaranteed for principal and interest by the full faith and credit of the U.S. government and, as of September 30, 2008, totaled about $2.7 trillion, of which the Social Security trust funds held about $2.4 trillion. Additional information regarding Social Security and Medicare programs are included in the annual reports of the Trustees of the Social Security and Medicare trust funds; the summary and full annual reports can be found on Social Security's website at http://www.socialsecurity.gov/OACT/TR/index.html.

Readers can use this statement to find such information as

- the total amount of projected additional resources needed today, under current policy, in addition to future earmarked revenue for the federal government to fund the major social insurance programs over the projected period, and
- how much the projected resource needs have changed from prior years.

For example, in 2008, Social Security's projected expenditures of about $43 trillion exceeded projected revenue of about $36 trillion by approximately $7 trillion.

Estimated amounts shown as needed over an infinite period, while not shown on the Statement of Social Insurance, are presented in the Supplemental Information section of the CFR. The present value of the resources needed for programs noted above totaled about $102 trillion based on an infinite time period.

Illustrative Social Insurance Information

Present Value of Long-Range (75 Years) Actuarial Projections	**As of January 1**				
	Unaudited				
(In billions of dollars)	**2008**	**2007**	**2006**	**2005**	**2004**
• **Federal Old-Age, Survivors and Disability Insurance (Social Security)**					
Revenue (Contributions and Earmarked Taxes)	36,357	34,113	32,107	29,450	27,699
Expenditures for Scheduled Future Benefits	(42,911)	(40,876)	(38,557)	(35,154)	(32, 928)
Present Value of Future Expenditures in Excess of Future Revenue	(6,555)	(6,763)	(6,449)	(5,704)	(5,229)

Present Value of Long-Range (75 Years) Actuarial Projections	As of January 1				
	Unaudited				
(In billions of dollars)	**2008**	**2007**	**2006**	**2005**	**2004**
■ **Federal Hospital Insurance (Medicare Part A)**					
Revenue (Contributions and Earmarked Taxes)	11,883	11,023	10,644	9,435	8,976
Expenditures for Scheduled Future Benefits	(24,619)	(23,315)	(21,934)	(18,264)	(17,468)
Present Value of Future Expenditures in Excess of Future Revenue	(12,736)	(12,292)	(11,290)	(8,829)	(8,492)
▲ **Federal Supplementary Medical Insurance (Medicare Part B)**					
Revenue (Premiums)	5,478	4,789	4,481	4,187	3,889
Expenditures for Scheduled Future Benefits	*(21,197)*	*(18,221)*	*(17,613)*	*(16,571)*	*(15,329)*
Present Value of Future Expenditures in Excess of Future Revenue	*(15,719)*	*(13,432)*	*(13,131)*	*(12,384)*	*(11, 440)*
▲ **Federal Supplementary Medical Insurance (Medicare Part D)**					
Revenue (Premiums and State Transfers)	2,107	2,405	2,366	2,547	2,651
Expenditures for Scheduled Future Benefits	(9,964)	(10,766)	(10,250)	(11,233)	(10,770)
Present Value of Future Expenditures in Excess of Future Revenue	(7,857)	(8,361)	(7,884)	(8,686)	(8,119)
Other - Present Value of Future Expenditures in Excess of Future Revenue	(104)	(100)	(97)	(86)	(83)
Total	(42,970)	(40,948)	(38,851)	(35,689)	(33,363)

- **Social Security** provides **Federal Old-Age and Survivors Insurance and Disability Insurance.** Both programs are financed by taxes on employees and employers, including the self-employed, and are administered by the Social Security Administration.

■ **Federal Hospital Insurance (Medicare Part A)** covers inpatient hospital and related care. It is financed primarily by a payroll tax on employers and employees, including the self-employed, and a portion of the income taxes paid on Social Security benefits. Federal Hospital Insurance is administered by the Department of Health and Human Services.

▲ **Federal Supplementary Medical Insurance,** which also is administered by the Department of Health and Human Services, consists of two parts, called Medicare Part B and Medicare Part D. Medicare Part B covers hospital outpatient services, physicians' services, and other assorted products and services. Part D covers the federal government's prescription drug program. Both parts are financed primarily by transfers from the general fund of the Treasury and premiums from participants.

NOTES TO THE FINANCIAL STATEMENTS

The notes to the financial statements are an important source of information about the financial operations and condition of the federal government. As stated on the bottom of each of the statements, notes are considered an integral part of the financial statements. Moreover, most of the consolidated financial statements contain references to one or more notes.

The 25 notes to the federal government's fiscal year 2008 consolidated financial statements provided 73 pages of important and required disclosures. The notes addressed the following topics:

1. Significant Accounting Policies	10. Accounts Payable	19. Contingencies
2. Cash and Other Monetary Assets	11. Federal Debt Securities Held by the Public	20. Commitments
3. Accounts and Taxes Receivable	12. Federal Employee and Veteran Benefits Payable	21. Earmarked Funds
4. Loans Receivable and Loan Guarantee Liabilities	13. Environmental and Disposal Liabilities	22. Indian Trust Funds
5. Inventories and Related Property	14. Benefits Due and Payable	23. Social Insurance
6. Property, Plant and Equipment	15. Insurance Program Liabilities	24. Stewardship Land and Heritage Assets
7. Securities and Investments	16. Other Liabilities	25. Subsequent Events
8. Financial and Housing Market Stabilization	17. Collections and Refunds of Federal Revenue	
9. Other Assets	18. Prior Period Adjustments	

The first note to the federal government's consolidated financial statements summarizes the significant accounting policies used in accounting for and reporting on the federal government's consolidated financial information. Other notes provide important disclosures and details about the items on the statements. For example, the Federal Employee and Veteran Benefits Payable note provides details about the composition of benefits payable to federal civilian employees and military personnel and disabled veterans, which exceeded $5.3 trillion as of September 30, 2008. Because this estimated amount is based on actuarial calculations, the note also identifies the significant long-term assumptions used in determining these liabilities and related expenses. In addition, the note discloses that the Department of Veterans Affairs (VA) provides medical care to veterans on an "as available" basis, subject to the limits of the annual appropriations. VA does not report an accrued long-term actuarial liability for this medical care, but recognizes the medical care expenses in the period the services are provided. For the time period 2004 through 2008, the note states that the average medical cost per year was $30 billion. Further, the note discloses that VA provides pension benefits to certain veterans and their dependents based on annual eligibility reviews. Although VA does not recognize a long-term actuarial liability for these pension benefits, VA discloses the projected amounts of future payments for pension benefits, $97.3 billion as of September 30, 2008, and $81.4 billion as of September 30, 2007. Readers can use this information to learn which benefit programs are primarily responsible for changes in the federal government's liability to its civilian employees, military personnel, and veterans, and thus, to better understand factors likely to drive future federal disbursements.

Illustrative Note Information

Federal Employee and Veteran Benefits Payable as of September 30						
(In billions of dollars)	**Civilian**		**Military**		**Total**	
	2008	**2007**	**2008**	**2007**	**2008**	**2007**
Pension and accrued benefits	1,454.8	1,386.3	1,154.1	1,028.8	2,608.9	2,415.1
Post-retirement health and accrued benefits	341.8	311.6	820.6	835.9	1,162.4	1,147.5
Veteran compensation and burial benefits	N/A	N/A	1,466.7	1,127.7	1,466.7	1,127.7
Liabilities for other benefits	54.5	52.3	26.4	26.5	80.9	78.8
Total	1,851.1	1,750.2	3,467.8	3,018.9	5,318.9	4,769.1

The table below is the summary table from the fiscal year 2008 note for Federal Employee and Veteran Benefits Payable, which shows how much the federal government estimates it owes civilian and military employees in various categories of benefits. The full note also provides additional tables depicting the details of the changes in the pension and post-retirement health benefits categories from fiscal year 2007 to fiscal year 2008 for both civilian and military employees, and discusses the various categories.

SUPPLEMENTAL INFORMATION

The Supplemental Information section is intended to provide additional information to enhance the understanding of the federal government's operations or financial condition. The supplemental information is not required to be audited.

Readers can use this section to understand

- how Medicare and Social Security Trust Funds are financed, and the sustainability of Social Security and the Hospital Insurance Fund (Medicare Part A) under current law. For example, Medicare Part A is used to pay for inpatient hospital stays, skilled nursing care, hospice, and certain home health services. This trust fund is financed primarily through payroll taxes and in 2008 was projected to remain solvent until 2019. Similarly, the combined Social Security Trust Funds are financed primarily through payroll taxes and in 2008 were projected to remain solvent until 2041. Actuarial projections of the solvency of these trust funds are updated annually.
- the sensitivity of changes in the assumptions used to determine estimated cashflow projections for these trust funds. For example, the Social Security Trust Funds used assumptions such as the changes in the average annual reduction in death rates, fertility rates, and net immigration to determine the present values of estimated future expenditures in excess of future revenue.
- the current year's net results for Medicare and Social Security Trust Funds, which is computed as revenue received from payroll and benefit taxes and insurance premiums less expenditures for health care and income security benefits.

- the estimated cost of maintenance needed to bring property owned by the federal government to an acceptable condition, called deferred maintenance (e.g., for fiscal year 2008, the estimated cost of deferred maintenance on such property ranged from about $110 billion to approximately $117 billion).
- the amount of federal taxes paid by individuals grouped by income level (e.g., individuals with adjusted gross incomes of $200,000 or more paid about 53 percent of the individual federal income taxes collected for tax year 2006).

The following table is taken from the Supplemental Information section of the CFR. It is intended to provide additional information about individual taxable income and taxes paid. Although the data are from the 2006 tax year, the information nonetheless helps readers understand how the federal tax burden is distributed based on adjusted gross income.

Illustrative Supplemental Information

Individual Income Tax Liability for Tax Year 2006						
Adjusted gross income (AGI)	**Number of taxable returns**	**AGI**	**Total income tax**	**Average AGI per return**	**Average income tax per return**	**Income tax as a Percentage of AGI**
	(in thousands)	(in millions of dollars)	(in millions of dollars)	(in whole dollars)	(in whole dollars)	
Under $15,000	37,614	188,624	3,141	5,015	84	1.7%
$15,000 to under $30,000	29,649	655,386	22,562	22,105	761	3.4%
$30,000 to under $50,000	24,907	973,569	59,846	39,088	2,403	6.1%
$50,000 to under $100,000	30,053	2,123,894	185,019	70,672	6,156	8.7%
$100,000 to under $200,000	12,110	1,610,028	210,538	132,956	17,386	13.1%
$200,000 or more	4,088	2,431,160	545,226	594,740	133,380	22.4%
Total	138,421	7,982,661	1,026,332			

STEWARDSHIP INFORMATION

The Stewardship Information section of the CFR describes how much the federal government spent for programs that provide long-term benefits to the public, or stewardship investments. These programs include grants for construction and major renovation of state and local government property, such as bridges and roads, and grants for education and training. The Stewardship Information section also describes the expenses the federal government has incurred in its basic and applied research and in development programs. The Stewardship Information section is not required to be audited.

Readers can use this section to find such information as

- how much the federal government spent on nonfederal physical property such as state and local bridges and roads, and whether such spending has increased or decreased,
- how much the federal government spent on educating and training the public and whether such spending has increased or decreased, and
- how much the federal government spent on research and development, and whether such spending has increased or decreased.

The next illustrative table on stewardship investments, reports annual expenditures from fiscal year 2004 through fiscal year 2008. It includes items that the government considers investments in the future of the nation, such as public education and training—reported under investments in human capital, and various categories of research and development. The amounts reported for fiscal years 2004–2007 are restated due to agencies' continued reviewing, correcting, and updating these data.

Government Accountability Office Report

GAO's report tells readers whether or not, or to what extent, the information provided in the CFS is reliable. GAO conducts its audit of the CFS in accordance with U.S. generally accepted government auditing standards, and obtains and evaluates evidence, with the objective of providing a formal written conclusion on whether the consolidated financial statements taken as a whole are presented fairly, in all material respects, in conformity with U.S. generally accepted accounting principles. The Citizen's Guide,

MD&A, Supplemental, and Stewardship Information sections in the CFR are not required to be audited.

The auditor may express an **unqualified opinion**, a **qualified opinion**, or an **adverse opinion**, or **disclaim an opinion** on the fairness of the financial statements taken as a whole. In an **unqualified opinion**, the auditor states that the information in the financial statements and accompanying notes is presented fairly, in all material respects, in conformity with U.S. generally accepted accounting principles. A **qualified opinion** discloses exceptions to an unqualified opinion, such as inadequate disclosures or selected nonconformities with U.S. generally accepted accounting principles. However, in a qualified opinion, the exceptions are not considered material enough to affect the fairness of the statements taken as a whole. Exceptions considered too serious or pervasive to justify a qualified opinion result in an **adverse opinion**, which states that the financial statements taken as a whole are not presented fairly, in all material respects, in conformity with U.S. generally accepted accounting principles. The circumstances related to such exceptions are also disclosed in the auditor's report. A **disclaimer of opinion** may result when the auditor is unable to obtain sufficient information upon which to base an opinion. The circumstances related to a disclaimer are described in the auditor's report.

Illustrative Stewardship Information

Stewardship Investments for the Years Ended September 30					
	Fiscal year	**Restated fiscal year**	**Restated fiscal year**	**Restated fiscal year**	**Restated fiscal year**
(In billions of dollars)	**2008**	**2007**	**2006**	**2005**	**2004**
Investments in nonfederal physical property	57.8	56.2	54.4	51.9	54.8
Investments in human capital	77.2	76.1	107.4	88.2	76.6
Research and development					
Investments in basic research	27.6	26.5	25.2	25.1	23.4
Investments in applied research	21.4	22.2	21.7	21.2	20.0
Investments in development	79.2	66.3	52.1	42.1	37.9
Total investments	263.2	247.3	260.8	228.5	212.7

GAO expressed an unqualified opinion on the 2008 and 2007 Statements of Social Insurance. GAO disclaimed an opinion on the fiscal year 2008 and 2007 Consolidated Financial Statements other than the Statements of Social Insurance because of the effects of persistent material weaknesses in the federal government's internal control and certain accounting and reporting practices that limited the scope of work that could be performed; a major factor in this limitation is the Department of Defense's continued inability to undergo an audit of its financial statements.

GAO's report also includes an opinion on whether the federal government had effective internal control over financial reporting and over compliance with laws and regulations. It also reports on any identified significant matters of noncompliance with selected provisions of applicable laws and regulations. For fiscal year 2008, GAO reported that the federal government did not maintain effective internal control over financial reporting (including safeguarding assets) and compliance with significant laws and regulations. GAO's work to test compliance with selected provisions of significant laws and regulations in fiscal year 2008 was limited by material weaknesses and scope limitations. GAO's audit report would not be possible without the commitment and professionalism of Inspectors General throughout the federal government who are responsible for annually auditing the financial statements of individual federal agencies.

How the Federal Government's Accrual-Basis Consolidated Financial Statements Relate to One Another

The federal government's consolidated financial statements consist of (1) five interrelated statements, referred to as the accrual-basis consolidated financial statements, and (2) the Statement of Social Insurance, which does not relate to the other consolidated financial statements. The chart on the next page provides an overview of the five accrual-basis consolidated financial statements and how selected components of those statements are related.

- ▲ The total operating expense, called Net Cost, presented in the Statement of Net Cost is used in the Statement of Operations and Changes in Net Position to determine whether the federal government's financial operations (revenue less expenses) resulted in net operating cost or net operating revenue for the year.

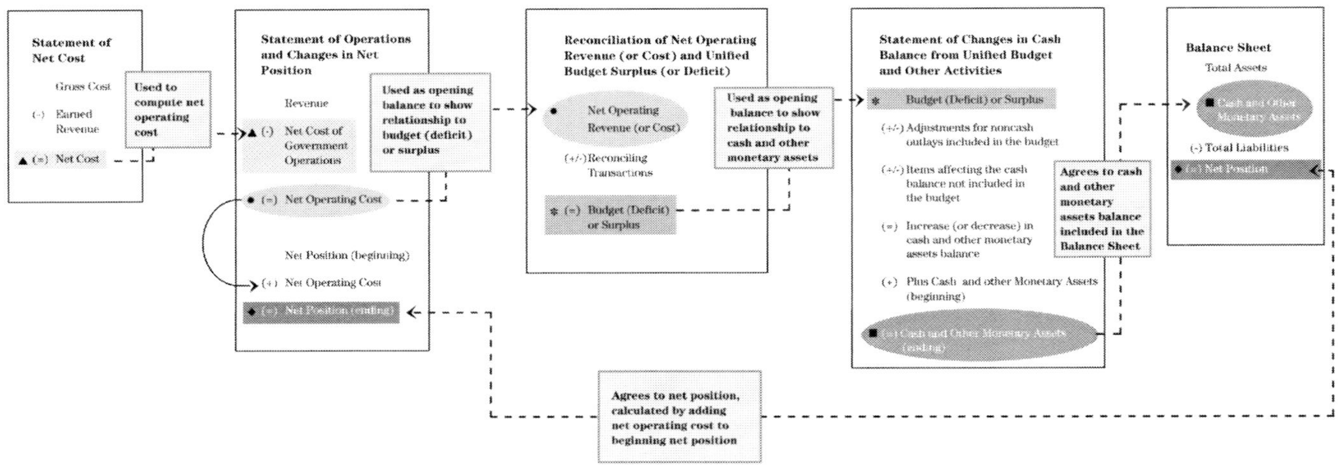

Statement of Net Cost
Gross Cost
(-) Earned Revenue
(=) Net Cost
Used to compute net operating cost
Statement of Operations and Changes in Net Position
Revenue
(-) Net Cost of Government Operations
(=) Net Operating Cost
Net Position (beginning)
(+) Net Operating Cost
(=) Net Position (ending)
Used as opening balance to show relationship to budget (deficit) or surplus
Reconciliation of Net Operating Revenue (or Cost) and Unified Budget Surplus (or Deficit)
Net Operating Revenue (or Cost)
(+/-) Reconciling Transactions
(=) Budget (Deficit) or Surplus
Used as opening balance to show relationship to cash and other monetary assets
Statement of Changes in Cash Balance from Unified Budget and Other Activities
Budget (Deficit) or Surplus
(+/-) Adjustments for noncash outlays included in the budget
(+/-) Items affecting the cash balance not included in the budget
(=) Increase (or decrease) in cash and other monetary assets balance
(+) Plus Cash and other Monetary Assets (beginning)
(=) Cash and Other Monetary Assets (ending)
Agrees to cash and other monetary assets balance included in the Balance Sheet
Balance Sheet
Total Assets
Cash and Other Monetary Assets
(-) Total Liabilities
(=) Net Position
Agrees to net position, calculated by adding net operating cost to beginning net position

- ● The operating result from the Statement of Operations and Changes in Net Position explains the change in the federal government's net position. It is also the beginning balance in the Reconciliation of Net Operating Revenue (or Cost) and Unified Budget Surplus (or Deficit).
- ♦ The Net Position from the Statement of Operations and Changes in Net Position agrees to the Net Position on the Balance Sheet, which is based on the difference between the federal government's reported assets and liabilities.
- ❊ The unified budget result is used in the Reconciliation of Net Operating Revenue (or Cost) and Unified Budget Surplus (or Deficit) and the Statement of Changes in Cash Balance from Unified Budget and Other Activities to show how the federal government's financial operations and changes in cash and other monetary assets are connected to the unified budget results.
- ■ The federal government's ending cash and other monetary assets balance from the Statement of Changes in Cash Balance from Unified Budget and Other Activities is the same as the "cash and other monetary assets" line on the Balance Sheet.

In: Federal Financial Reporting
Editor: Denise Mahoney
ISBN: 978-1-62948-871-4

Chapter 3

A CITIZEN'S GUIDE TO THE 2012 FINANCIAL REPORT OF THE UNITED STATES GOVERNMENT*

U.S. Department of the Treasury

The Citizen's Guide (Guide) to the Fiscal Year (FY) 2012 Financial Report of the U.S. Government summarizes the current financial position and condition of the U.S. Government (See "Where We Are Now", p. ii) and discusses key financial topics, including fiscal sustainability (See "Where We Are Headed", p. v). This Guide and the Financial Report of the U.S. Government are produced by the U.S. Department of the Treasury in cooperation with the Office of Management and Budget (OMB). The Secretary of the Treasury, Deputy Director for Management of OMB, and Comptroller General of the United States at the Government Accountability Office (GAO) believe that the information discussed in this Guide is important to all Americans.

* This is an edited, reformatted and augmented version of a U.S. Department of the Treasury Report.

WHERE WE ARE NOW

Comparing the Budget and the Financial Report

The ***Budget of the United States Government*** (Budget) is the Government's primary financial planning and control tool. It accounts for past Government receipts and spending, and presents the President's proposed receipt and spending plan. The Budget compares *receipts*, or cash received by the Government, with *outlays*, or payments made by the Government to the public, to derive a budget *surplus* (excess of receipts over outlays) or *deficit* (excess of outlays over receipts). Receipts and outlays are measured generally based on when the Government receives or dispenses cash.

The ***Financial Report of the United States Government*** (*Report*) focuses on the Government's revenues and costs (what came in and what went out), assets and liabilities (what it owns and owes), and other important financial information. It compares *revenues* (what the Government has collected and expects to collect, but has not necessarily received), with its *costs* (what the Government has incurred, but has not necessarily paid) to derive net operating cost. Chart 1 compares the Government's budget deficit and net operating cost for FY 2008-2012. The difference between the $1.1 trillion budget deficit and $1.3 trillion net operating cost in FY 2012 is predominantly due to: (1) non-cash costs associated with an increase in estimated liabilities related to Federal employee and veteran benefits, and (2) a partially offsetting decrease in costs associated with lower projected liabilities to the Government-Sponsored Enterprises (GSEs), specifically Fannie Mae and Freddie Mac. Together, the Budget and the chapter present complementary perspectives on the Government's financial position and condition, and provide a valuable decision-making and management tool for the Nation's leaders.

What Came in and What Went Out

What came in? Chart 2 shows that increases in each of the three revenue categories (individual income tax and withholdings, corporate income taxes, and other revenue) combined to increase total Government revenues by $154.4 billion (6.5 percent) to just over $2.5 trillion for FY 2012. Together, individual and corporate taxes accounted for about 86 percent of total revenues. Other revenues include excise and unemployment taxes, and customs duties.

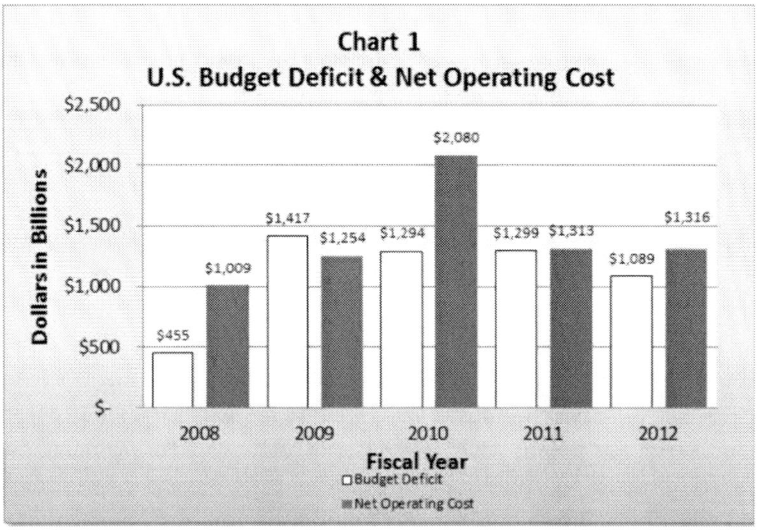

Chart 1.

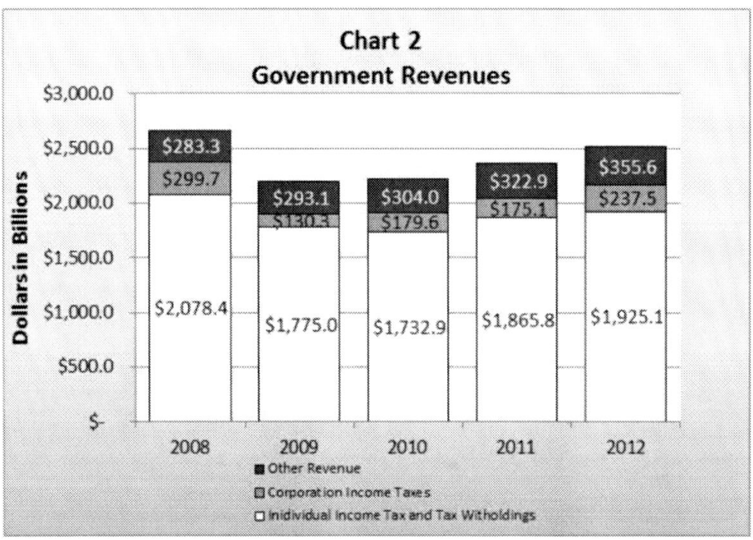

Chart 2.

What went out? The Government derives its net cost ($3.8 trillion in FY 2012) by subtracting revenues earned from Government programs (e.g., Medicare premiums, National park entry fees, and postal fees) from its gross costs and adjusts the amount for gains or losses from changes in actuarial assumptions used to estimate future liabilities for Federal employee and veteran benefits. The Government deducts taxes and other revenues shown in Chart 2, as well as adjustments for unmatched transactions and balances, from its net cost to arrive at its "bottom line" net operating cost, which increased by $3.7 billion (less than one-half of one percent), to remain essentially unchanged at $1.3 trillion in FY 2012. However, this minimal change includes significant offsetting changes, primarily: (1) a $292.1 billion increase in certain cost estimates for federal employee and veteran benefits; and (2) a $288.7 billion cost decrease[1] associated with changes in Government liabilities to the GSEs.

Chart 3 shows that the largest contributors to the Government's net cost in FY 2012, as is the case in most years, include the Departments of Health and Human Services (HHS) and Defense (DoD) and the Social Security Administration (SSA). The bulk of HHS and SSA costs come from major social insurance and postemployment benefits programs administered by those agencies (e.g., Medicare for HHS, and Social Security for SSA). While much of DoD's total costs relate to military operations and personnel, most of the increase in DoD's cost during FY 2012 was attributed to its Military Retirement Fund and other benefits programs.

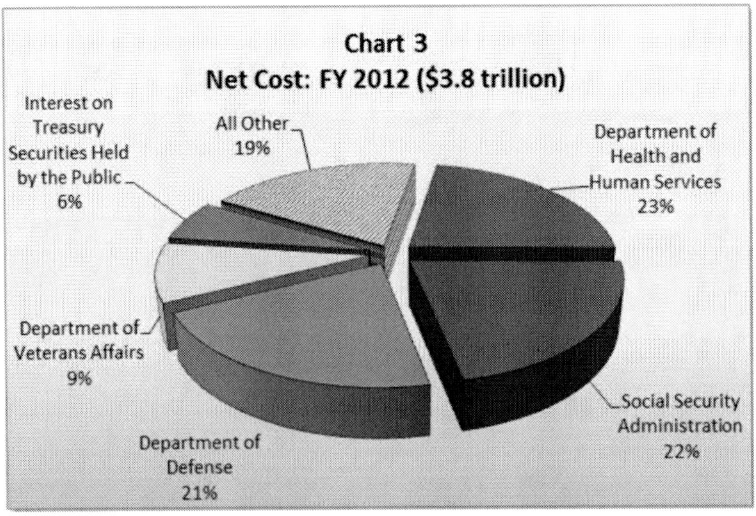

Chart 3.

What We Own and What We Owe

Chart 4 is a summary of what the Government owns in assets and what it owes in liabilities. As of September 30, 2012, the Government held about $2.7 trillion in assets, comprised mostly of net property, plant, and equipment ($855.0 billion) and a combined total of $1,009.1 billion in net loans receivable (e.g., student loans) and direct loans and investments associated with the Troubled Asset Relief Program (TARP) and the GSEs (which relate to the Government's economic recovery efforts). In recent years, with the ongoing wind-down of these programs, the balances of many of these investments have declined primarily through repayments and sales. Beyond these assets, other significant resources are available to the Government, including stewardship assets, such as natural resources, and the Government's power to tax and set monetary policy.

The $18.8 trillion in total liabilities is comprised mostly of: (1) $11.3 trillion in Federal debt securities held by the public and accrued interest[2] and (2) $6.3 trillion in Federal employee and veteran benefits payable. The Government also reports about $4.9 trillion of intragovernmental debt outstanding, which arises when one part of the Government borrows from another. For example, Government funds (e.g., Social Security and Medicare trust funds) are typically required to invest excess annual receipts in Federal debt securities issued by the Treasury Department, thus creating liabilities of the Treasury and assets of the trust funds. These respective amounts are included in individual Treasury Department and investing agency financial statements, but offset each other when the Governmentwide consolidated financial statements are prepared.

The sum of debt held by the public and intragovernmental debt equals gross Federal debt, which, with some adjustments, is subject to a statutory ceiling (i.e., the debt limit), which was most recently raised by $1.2 trillion to $16.394 trillion in January 2012 pursuant to the Budget Control Act (BCA) of 2011. As of September 30, 2012, the Government's total debt outstanding subject to the debt limit was $16.027 trillion, $367 billion below the current limit. As budget deficits continue to occur, the Government will have to borrow more from the public. Instances where the debt held by the public increases faster than the economy[3] for extended periods can pose additional challenges.

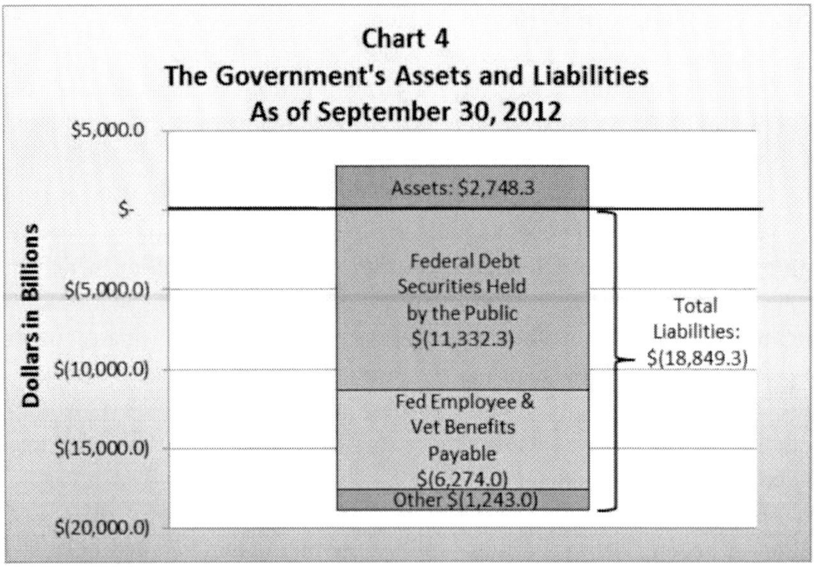

Chart 4.

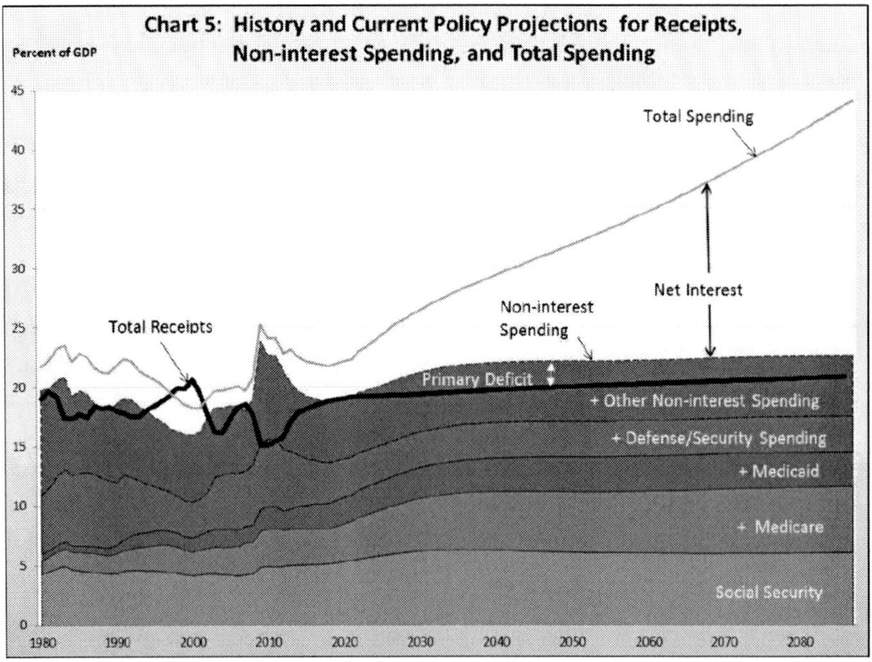

Chart 5.

WHERE WE ARE HEADED

An important purpose of this Guide and the chapter is to help citizens understand current fiscal policy, and the importance and magnitude of policy reforms necessary to make it sustainable. A sustainable policy is one where the ratio of debt held by the public to Gross Domestic Product (GDP) (the debt-to-GDP ratio) is ultimately stable or declining. To determine if current fiscal policy is sustainable, the projections discussed in this Guide assume current policy will be sustained indefinitely and draw out the implications for the growth of the debt-to-GDP ratio.[4] The projections are therefore neither forecasts nor predictions. As policy changes are enacted, then actual financial outcomes will, of course, be different than those projected.

The projections presented in this chapter were finalized prior to the enactment of the American Taxpayer Relief Act (ATRA) in January 2013.[5]

Receipts, Spending, and the Debt

Chart 5 shows historical and current policy projections for receipts, non-interest spending by major category, and total spending expressed as a percent of GDP. The difference between the receipts and non-interest spending shares of GDP - the primary deficit-to-GDP ratio, grew rapidly in 2009 due to the financial crisis and the recession, and the Federal Government's response. The ratio stayed large from 2010 to 2012 despite shrinking in each successive year, but is projected to fall rapidly between 2013 and 2018 as the economy recovers and spending reductions called for in the BCA take effect, reaching primary balance in 2018, and remaining relatively flat and near zero until 2021. Between 2022 and 2039, however, increased spending for Social Security and health programs[6] due to continued aging of the population and anticipated rising health costs is expected to cause the primary deficit-to-GDP ratio to steadily deteriorate, reaching 2.3 percent of GDP in 2039. After 2039, the ratio is projected to slowly decline to 1.7 percent of GDP in 2087 as the impact of the baby boom generation retiring dissipates. In these projections, the Affordable Care Act (ACA) [7] provision of health insurance subsidies and expanded Medicaid coverage boost federal spending, and other provisions significantly reduce per-beneficiary Medicare and Medicaid cost growth. Overall, the ACA is projected to substantially reduce federal expenditures over the next 75 years. However, as noted in the chapter, there is uncertainty about the effectiveness of the ACA's provisions designed to reduce health care cost growth. Even if those provisions work as intended and as assumed in these projections, Chart 5 still shows a persistent gap between projected receipts and total non-interest spending.

The primary deficit projections in Chart 5, along with those for interest rates and GDP, determine the debt-to-GDP ratio projections shown in Chart 6. That ratio was 73 percent at the end of FY 2012 and under current policy is projected to grow to 78 percent in 2022, 145 percent in 2042, and 395 percent in 2087. While these projections are subject to considerable uncertainty, the debt- to-GDP ratio would continue to rise unsustainably under current policy.

The Fiscal Gap and the Cost of Delaying Policy Reform

It is estimated that preventing the debt-to-GDP ratio from rising over the next 75 years would require some combination of expenditure reductions and revenue increases that amount, on average, to 2.7 percent of GDP over each of the next 75 years. The timing of changes to non- interest spending and receipts that close this "75-year fiscal gap" has important implications for the well-being of future generations. For example, relative to a policy that begins immediately, it is estimated that the magnitude of reforms necessary to close the 75-year fiscal gap increases by nearly 20 percent if action is delayed by 10-years and for more than 50 percent if action is delayed 20 years.

Conclusion

The Government took potentially significant steps towards fiscal sustainability by enacting: (1) the ACA in 2010 and (2) the BCA in 2011. The ACA holds the prospect of lowering the long-term per beneficiary spending growth for Medicare and Medicaid, and the BCA significantly curtails discretionary spending. Together, these two laws substantially reduce the estimated long-term fiscal gap. But even with these new laws, the Government's debt-to-GDP ratio is projected to increase continuously over the next 75 years and beyond if current policy is kept in place, which implies that current policy is not sustainable. Subject to the important caveat that changes in policy not be so abrupt that they slow the economy's recovery, the sooner policies are put in place to avert these trends, the smaller the revenue increases and/or spending decreases will need to be to return the Government to a sustainable fiscal path.[8]

THE NATION BY THE NUMBERS

The chapter provides the President, Congress, and the American people a comprehensive view of how the Government is managing taxpayer dollars. It discusses the Government's financial position and condition, its revenues and costs, assets and liabilities, and other responsibilities and commitments, as well as important financial issues that affect the Nation and its citizens both now and in the future. The table on the following page presents several key indicators of the Government's financial position and condition, which are summarized in this Guide and discussed in greater detail in the chapter.

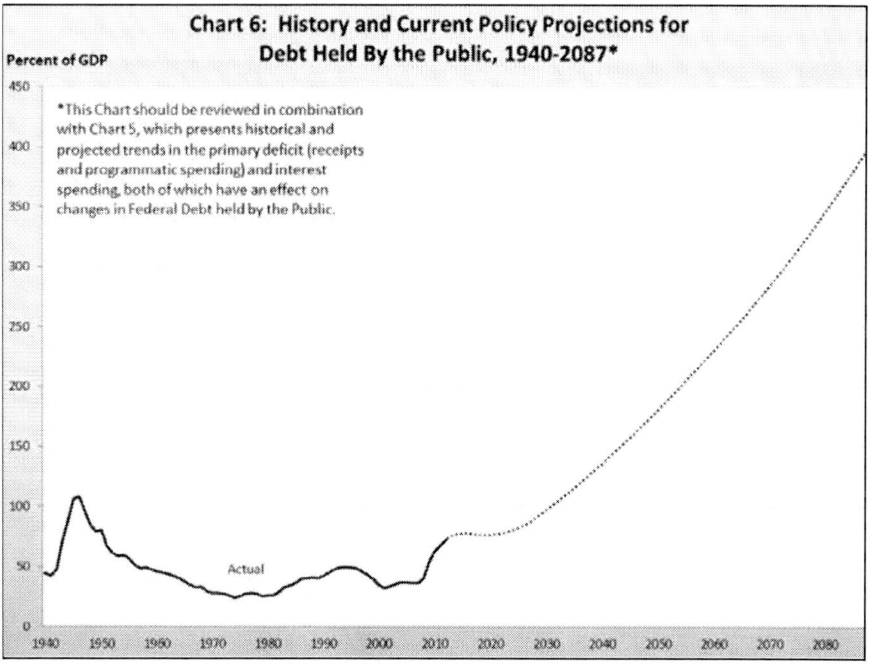

Chart 6.

NATION BY THE NUMBERS

A Snapshot of The Government's Financial Position & Condition

billions of dollars	2012	2011
Gross Costs	**$ (3,844.9)**	**$ (3,998.3)**
Less: Earned Revenues	$350.8	$ 365.6
Gain/(Loss) from Changes in Assumptions	$ (320.2)	$ (28.1)
Net Cost	**$ (3,814.3)**	**$ (3,660.8)**
Less: Total Taxes and Other Revenues	**$2,518.2**	**$2,363.8**
Unmatched Transactions and Balances	$ (20.2)	$ (15.6)
Net Operating Cost	**$ (1,316.3)**	**$ (1,312.6)**
Assets:	**$2,748.3**	**$ 2,707.3**
Less: Liabilities, comprised of:		
Debt Held By the Public & Accrued Interest	$ (11,332.3)	$ (10,174.1)
Federal Employee & Veteran Benefits	$ (6,274.0)	$ (5,792.2)
Other	$ (1,243.0)	$ (1,526.4)
Total Liabilities	**$ (18,849.3)**	**$ (17,492.7)**
Net Position (Assets Minus Liabilities)	**$ (16,101.0)**	**$ (14,785.4)**
Sustainability Measures:		
Social Insurance Net Expenditures[1]	$ (38,554)	$ (33,830)
Total Non-Interest Net Expenditures[2]	$ (16,500)	$ (6,400)
Sustainability Measures as Percent of Gross Domestic Product (GDP):		
Social Insurance Net Expenditures[3]	-4.2%	-3.8%
Total Federal Government Non-Interest Net Expenditures	-1.7%	-0.7%
Budget Results		
Unified Budget Deficit	$ (1,089.4)	**$ (1,298.6)**

[1] Source: Statement of Social Insurance. Amounts equal present value of projected revenues and expenditures for scheduled benefits over the next 75 years of certain benefit programs that are referred to as Social Insurance (e.g., Social Security, Medicare). Amounts represent 'open group' population (all current and future beneficiaries). These amounts are not considered liabilities on the balance sheet.

[2] Represents the 75-year projection of the Federal Government's receipts less non-interest spending as reported in the 'Statement of Long Term Fiscal Projections' in the Required Supplementary Information section of the Financial Report of the U.S. Government .

[3] GDP values used represent the average of 75-year present value of nominal GDP for 2012 and 2011 from the Social Security and Medicare Trustees Reports.

The Government Accountability Office's (GAO) audit report on the U.S. Government's consolidated financial statements can be found beginning on page 223 of the full *Report.* GAO disclaimed an opinion on the 2012, 2011, and 2010 Statements of Social Insurance (SOSI) and the 2012 and 2011 Statements of Changes in Social Insurance Amounts because of significant uncertainties (discussed in Note 26 in the chapter) primarily related to the achievement of projected reductions in Medicare cost growth reflected in the 2012, 2011, and 2010 SOSI. However, GAO issued an unqualified or "clean" opinion on the 2009 and 2008 SOSI. 9 In addition, certain material financial reporting control weaknesses and other limitations on the scope of its work prevented GAO from expressing an opinion on the remaining FY 2012 and 2011 financial statements in the chapter.

FIND OUT MORE

The *2012 Financial Report of the United States Government* and other information about the Nation's finances are available at:

- U.S. Department of the Treasury, http://www.fms.treas.gov/fr.html;
- OMB's Office of Federal Financial Management, http://www.whitehouse.gov/omb/financial/index.html; and
- GAO, http://www.gao.gov/financial.html.

End Notes

[1] Department of the Treasury's FY 2012 Annual Financial Report, p. 101.

[2] Debt held by the public and accrued interest, as reported on the Government's balance sheet, primarily consists of Treasury securities, net of unamortized discounts and premiums, and accrued interest. The "public" consists of individuals, corporations, state and local governments, Federal Reserve Banks, foreign governments, and other entities outside the Federal Government.

[3] Considering key macroeconomic indicators can help place the discussion of the Government's financial results in a broader context. During FY 2012, the economy continued to grow, and at a faster rate than the previous year, job creation accelerated, and the unemployment rate declined. These and other economic and financial developments are discussed in greater detail in the chapter.

[4] Current policy in the projections is based on current law, but includes extension of certain policies that expire under current law but are routinely extended or otherwise expected to continue, such as extension of relief from the Alternative Minimum Tax (AMT). In

addition, for this year's *Report*, the projections include the extension of all 2001/2003 tax cuts indefinitely, whereas in the FY 2011 *Report*, it was assumed that the high income tax cuts were allowed to expire.

[5] ATRA did not extend the 2001/2003 tax cuts for high income individuals and families that were assumed to occur in the projections. Updating the projections in this chapter to account for ATRA would therefore modestly reduce projected long term fiscal imbalances.

[6] The 2012 Medicare Trustees Report projects that, assuming full implementation of the Affordable Care Act (ACA) provisions, the Hospital Insurance (HI) Trust Fund will remain solvent under current law until 2024, at which point the share of estimated HI costs that could be paid from trust fund income is 87 percent, declining to 69 percent by 2086. As for Social Security, under current law, the Old-Age, Survivors, and Disability Insurance (OASDI) Trust Funds are projected to be exhausted in 2033, at which time the projected share of scheduled benefits payable from trust fund income is 75 percent, declining to 73 percent in 2086. The projections assume full Social Security and Medicare benefits are paid after the corresponding trust funds are exhausted. See http://www.ssa.gov/oact/trsum/index.html.

[7] The ACA refers to P.L. 111-148, as amended by P.L. 111-152. The ACA expands health insurance coverage, provides health insurance subsidies for low-income individuals and families, includes many measures designed to reduce health care cost growth, and significantly reduces Medicare payment rates.

[8] Further information about these fiscal projections and the underlying assumptions can be found in the Required Supplementary Information section of the Financial Report at www.fms.treas.gov/fr.

[9] In conformity with Federal accounting standards, Statements of Social Insurance are presented for the current year and each of the four preceding years.

In: Federal Financial Reporting
Editor: Denise Mahoney ISBN: 978-1-62948-871-4

Chapter 4

MANAGEMENT REPORT: IMPROVEMENTS NEEDED IN CONTROLS OVER THE PREPARATION OF THE U.S. CONSOLIDATED FINANCIAL STATEMENTS*

United States Government Accountability Office

WHY GAO DID THIS STUDY

Treasury, in coordination with OMB, prepares the *Financial Report of the United States Government*, which contains the CFS. Since GAO's first audit of the fiscal year 1997 CFS, certain material weaknesses and other limitations on the scope of its work have prevented GAO from expressing an opinion on the CFS, exclusive of the Statements of Social Insurance (SOSI). Also, GAO was unable to express opinions on the 2012, 2011, and 2010 SOSI and 2012 and 2011 Statements of Changes in Social Insurance Amounts because of significant uncertainties, primarily related to the achievement of projected reductions in Medicare cost growth, reflected in these statements. As part of

* This is an edited, reformatted and augmented version of the Highlights of GAO-13-540, a report to agency officials, dated June 2013.

the fiscal year 2012 CFS audit, GAO identified material weaknesses and other control deficiencies in the processes used to prepare the CFS. The purpose of this chapter is to (1) provide details on new control deficiencies GAO identified
related to the preparation of the CFS, (2) recommend improvements, and (3) provide the status of corrective actions taken by Treasury and OMB to address GAO's prior recommendations relating to the preparation of the CFS that remained open at the end of the fiscal year 2011 audit.

WHAT GAO RECOMMENDS

GAO is making six recommendations — five to Treasury and one to OMB— to address the new control deficiencies identified by GAO during the fiscal year 2012 CFS audit. In commenting on GAO's draft, OMB and Treasury generally concurred on 5 of the 6 recommendations, and Treasury will consider implementation of the other recommendation.

WHAT GAO FOUND

During its audit of the fiscal year 2012 consolidated financial statements of the U.S. government (CFS), GAO identified new and continuing control deficiencies in the Department of the Treasury's (Treasury) and the Office of Management and Budget's (OMB) processes used to prepare the CFS. These control deficiencies contributed to material weaknesses in internal control over the federal government's ability to

- adequately account for and reconcile intragovernmental activity and balances between federal entities;
- ensure that the federal government's accrual-based consolidated financial statements were (1) consistent with the underlying audited entities' financial statements, (2) properly balanced, and (3) in conformity with U.S. generally accepted accounting principles; and
- identify and either resolve or explain material differences between (1) components of the budget deficit that are used to prepare certain information in the CFS and (2) related amounts reported in federal

entities' financial statements and underlying financial information and records.

Specifically, for fiscal year 2012, GAO found that Treasury's procedures were not effectively designed to

- reasonably assure the timely submission of audited material line items for significant calendar year-end federal entities,
- determine the effect of restatements and reclassifications submitted by significant federal entities on related line items and notes presented in the CFS, and
- ensure that the budget statements included in the CFS were prepared in a reliable manner.

GAO also notified OMB of a reporting requirement in OMB Circular No. A-136, *Financial Reporting Requirements*, that may result in inconsistent and inaccurate reporting of compliance with the Federal Financial Management Improvement Act of 1996.

In addition, GAO found that various other control deficiencies identified in previous years' audits with respect to the CFS preparation continued to exist. Specifically, 31 of the 48 recommendations from GAO's prior reports regarding control deficiencies in the CFS preparation process remained open as of January 9, 2013, the date of GAO's report on its audit of the fiscal year 2012 CFS. GAO will continue to monitor the status of corrective actions taken to address the 6 new recommendations as well as the 31 open recommendations from prior years as part of its fiscal year 2013 CFS audit.

ABBREVIATIONS

CFO	chief financial officer
CFS	consolidated financial statements of the U.S. government
CSGL	Treasury's Central Standard General Ledger
FASAB	Federal Accounting Standards Advisory Board
FFMIA	Federal Financial Management Improvement Act
GAAP	generally accepted accounting principles
IRAS	Intragovernmental Reporting and Analysis System
OMB	Office of Management and Budget
SOP	standard operating procedure

SOSI	Statement of Social Insurance
STAR/CARS	Treasury's central accounting and reporting system

June 28, 2013

The Honorable Jacob J. Lew
Secretary of the Treasury

The Honorable Sylvia Mathews Burwell
Director
Office of Management and Budget

In our January 2013 report on the results of our audit of the consolidated financial statements of the U.S. government (CFS) for the fiscal years ended September 30, 2012 and 2011,[1,2] we disclaimed an opinion on the CFS, except for the 2009 and 2008 Statements of Social Insurance (SOSI), which received unqualified opinions.[3] Since GAO's first audit of the fiscal year 1997 CFS, certain material weaknesses in internal control over financial reporting and other limitations on the scope of our work have resulted in conditions that prevented us from expressing an opinion on the federal government's accrual-based consolidated financial statements.[4] These include material weaknesses that relate to the federal government's processes used to prepare the CFS.[5] Such material weaknesses involve the federal government's inability to

- adequately account for and reconcile intragovernmental activity and balances between federal entities;
- ensure that the federal government's accrual-based consolidated financial statements were (1) consistent with the underlying audited entities' financial statements, (2) properly balanced, and (3) in conformity with U.S. generally accepted accounting principles; and
- identify and either resolve or explain material differences between (1) certain components of the budget deficit reported in the Department of the Treasury's (Treasury) records that are used to prepare the Reconciliation of Net Operating Cost and Unified Budget Deficit, the Statement of Changes in Cash Balance from Unified Budget and Other Activities, and the Fiscal Projections for the U.S. Government (included in the unaudited Required Supplementary Information section of the *2012 Financial Report of the United States Government (Financial Report)*)[6] and (2) related amounts reported in federal

entities' financial statements and underlying financial information and records.

Treasury, in coordination with the Office of Management and Budget (OMB), prepares the CFS on behalf of the federal government.[7] Several of the material weaknesses in internal control over financial reporting that have contributed to our continuing disclaimers of opinion on the federal government's accrual-based consolidated financial statements were reported in detail along with related recommendations by other auditors in their audit reports on individual federal entities' financial statements.[8]

The purpose of this chapter is to provide (1) detailed information on new control deficiencies identified during our fiscal year 2012 audit that relate to the processes used by Treasury and OMB to prepare the CFS, (2) 6 recommendations to address these new control deficiencies, and (3) the status of corrective actions taken by Treasury and OMB to address the 48 recommendations relating to the processes used by them to prepare the CFS, detailed in our previous reports, that remained open at the end of the fiscal year 2011 audit.[9] In total, we closed 17 of the 48 recommendations at the end of the fiscal year 2012 audit. Of the 17 recommendations that have been closed, 7 were closed as a result of corrective actions taken by Treasury. We closed the other 10 recommendations by making 2 new recommendations in this chapter that are better aligned with the current status of the remaining internal control deficiencies associated with the budget statements included in the CFS and that reflect certain actions taken by Treasury. Appendix I provides a summary of the status of actions taken to address the open recommendations from our previous reports as of January 9, 2013, the date of our report on the audit of the fiscal year 2012 CFS.

SCOPE AND METHODOLOGY

As part of our audit of the fiscal years 2012 and 2011 CFS, we considered the federal government's financial reporting procedures and related internal control. Also, we determined the status of corrective actions taken by Treasury and OMB to address open recommendations relating to the processes used by them to prepare the CFS that were detailed in our previous reports. Based on the scope of our work and the effects of the other limitations on the scope of our audit noted throughout our audit report on the fiscal year 2012 CFS, our internal control work would not necessarily identify all deficiencies in internal control, including those that might be material weaknesses or significant deficiencies.[10] We have communicated each of the new control deficiencies to your staff. We performed our audit of the fiscal years 2012 and 2011 CFS in accordance with U.S. generally accepted government auditing standards. We believe that our audit provided a reasonable basis for our conclusions in this chapter.

We requested comments on a draft of this chapter from the Director of OMB and the Secretary of the Treasury or their designees. OMB provided oral comments, which are summarized in the Agency Comments and Our Evaluation section of this chapter. Treasury's Fiscal Assistant Secretary provided written comments on June 6, 2013, which are reprinted in their entirety in appendix II and are also summarized in the Agency Comments and Our Evaluation section.

NEW CONTROL DEFICIENCIES IDENTIFIED

During our audit of the fiscal year 2012 CFS, we identified several new internal control deficiencies in Treasury's and OMB's processes used to prepare the CFS. Specifically, we found that Treasury's procedures were not effectively designed to (1) reasonably assure the timely submission of audited material line items for significant calendar year-end federal entities, (2) determine the effect of restatements and reclassifications submitted by significant federal entities on related line items and notes presented in the CFS, and (3) ensure that the budget statements included in the CFS were prepared in a reliable manner. We also notified OMB of a reporting requirement in OMB Circular No. A-136, *Financial Reporting Requirements*,[11] that may result in inconsistent and inaccurate reporting of compliance with the Federal Financial Management Improvement Act of 1996 (FFMIA).[12]

Timely Submission of Audited Material Line Items for Significant Calendar Year-End Federal Entities

Treasury's procedures were not effectively designed to reasonably assure the timely submission of audited material line items for significant calendar year-end federal entities. Significant federal entities are required to submit a closing package to Treasury.[13] The closing package methodology is intended to link federal entities' audited consolidated department-level financial

statements to certain statements of the CFS. Chief financial officers (CFO) of significant federal entities are required to verify the consistency of the closing package data with their respective entities' audited financial statements. In addition, entity auditors are required to separately audit and report on the financial information in the closing packages. For the three significant federal entities with a calendar year-end of December 31, rather than a fiscal year-end of September 30, the entity auditors are only required to audit and report on the financial information in the closing packages that contributes material amounts to line items in the CFS, as identified by Treasury.[14]

Treasury's standard operating procedure (SOP) entitled "Significant Federal Entities Identification" includes procedures for Treasury to annually assess significant calendar year-end entities' financial statement line items to determine which line items are material to the *Financial Report*. Treasury's assessments are based on prior year financial information. The SOP also includes procedures for Treasury to notify OMB of changes in previously identified material line items. OMB is responsible for coordinating with each of the respective significant calendar year-end federal entities to obtain audit assurance over identified material line items through the closing package process.

During our audit of the fiscal year 2012 CFS, we found that Treasury's SOP did not include procedures to identify any material line items for significant calendar year-end entities that become material to the CFS during the current fiscal year, but that were not identified as material in the analysis using prior year financial information. In addition, we found that Treasury's SOP did not reasonably assure that identified material line items were audited as part of the significant calendar year-end entities' closing package process in the year a line item becomes material, including affording OMB adequate time to provide timely written notification to the significant calendar year-end entities of the line items that require audit coverage in the closing package process. *Standards for Internal Control in the Federal Government* provides that control activities are the policies, procedures, techniques, and mechanisms that enforce management's directives.[15] The standards also provide that agencies are to ensure accurate and timely recording of transactions. Without the above-noted procedures, Treasury and OMB are unable to reasonably assure that they have appropriate audit assurance over material financial information for all significant calendar year-end entity line items.

Recommendations for Executive Action

To help provide reasonable assurance that Treasury timely receives audited information for the material line items as part of the closing package process for the significant calendar year-end entities, we recommend that the Secretary of the Treasury direct the Fiscal Assistant Secretary, working in coordination with the Controller of OMB, to enhance the SOP entitled "Significant Federal Entities Identification" to include procedures for (1) identifying any material line items for significant calendar year-end entities that become material to the CFS during the current fiscal year but were not identified as material in the analysis using prior year financial information and (2) obtaining audit assurance over such identified material line items in the year they become material.

Analyzing Significant Federal Entities' Restatements and Reclassifications

Treasury's procedures were not effectively designed to determine the effect of restatements and reclassifications submitted by significant federal entities on related line items and notes presented in the CFS. Changes to amounts shown in previously issued financial statements can occur from restatements and reclassifications. A restatement is the process of revising previously issued financial statements to reflect the correction of an error in those financial statements. A reclassification is the movement of a prior year amount in comparative financial statements in order to conform to the current year presentation. Reclassifications can be from one line item to another, such as from inventory to other assets, or within components of a note to the financial statements. Significant federal entities that restate or reclassify their financial statements or notes are required to submit such changes to prior year amounts to Treasury as part of the entities' closing package.

Treasury's SOP entitled "Prior Period Adjustments" includes procedures for Treasury to analyze restatements and reclassifications submitted by the significant federal entities. During the preparation of the fiscal year 2012 CFS, Treasury analyzed the effect, in the aggregate, of restatements and reclassifications submitted by significant federal entities on the net position and net cost reported in the CFS for the prior fiscal year. Treasury determined that the effect was not material with respect to prior fiscal year net position and net cost at the government-wide level and, as such, adjustments to the prior year financial statements were not needed. However, we found that

Treasury's SOP did not include procedures to analyze whether the effect of federal entity-submitted restatements and reclassifications on related line items and notes presented in the CFS was material. *Standards for Internal Control in the Federal Government* provides that control activities are the policies, procedures, techniques, and mechanisms that enforce management's directives. The standards also provide that agencies are to ensure accurate and timely recording of transactions. Although we did not find any instances in our fiscal year 2012 audit, a material change in a line item or note related to significant federal entities' submitted restatements and reclassifications could occur and not be identified, resulting in inconsistent reporting between current and prior fiscal year amounts, which may mislead readers of the *Financial Report*.

Recommendation for Executive Action

To reasonably assure the comparability of the CFS between the current and prior fiscal year, we recommend that the Secretary of the Treasury direct the Fiscal Assistant Secretary to enhance the SOP entitled "Prior Period Adjustments" to include procedures for analyzing and assessing the effects of significant federal entities' restatements and reclassifications on related line items and notes presented in the CFS.

Preparation of the Budget Statements Included in the CFS

Treasury's procedures were not effectively designed to ensure that the CFS budget statements, which consist of the Reconciliation of Net Operating Cost and Unified Budget Deficit and Statement of Changes in Cash Balance from Unified Budget and Other Activities, were prepared in a reliable manner. Treasury uses a different approach for gathering federal entity data for the CFS budget statements than that of the closing package process used for the other CFS accrual-based financial statements. Specifically, the two CFS budget statements are not required statements at the federal entity level. As such, for these statements, Treasury uses the data, including the unified budget deficit amount (the difference between outlays and receipts) from its Central Summary General Ledger system (CSGL), which is unaudited.

During our audit of the fiscal year 2012 CFS, we found that although Treasury has made changes to its procedures and now documents its process for preparing the CFS budget statements, Treasury had not established and implemented effective processes and procedures to reconcile (1) outlays and receipts as recorded in the CSGL to outlays and receipts reported in the federal entities' audited financial statements and other financial data, (2) the operating results to the budget results, and (3) changes in cash and other monetary assets to the budget results. We identified several errors in the draft CFS budget statements that may have been prevented had these reconciliations been effectively completed. Further, both of the CFS budget statements had at least one line item that included amounts that were unsupported but were needed to make the statement balance. As a result, Treasury continues to be unable to demonstrate that it has fully identified and reported all items needed to adequately prepare the CFS budget statements.

The Federal Accounting Standards Advisory Board's Statement of Federal Financial Accounting Concepts No. 4, *Intended Audience and Qualitative Characteristics for the Consolidated Financial Report of the United States Government*, states that the consolidated financial report is a general purpose report that is aggregated from agency reports and tells users where to find information in other formats, both aggregated and disaggregated, such as individual agency reports, agency websites, and the President's Budget. Until Treasury is able to prepare the CFS budget statements in a manner that is fully consistent with the financial information from significant federal entities' audited financial statements, the CFS budget statements may not be reliable.

Recommendations for Executive Action

To improve the reliability of the information presented in the CFS budget statements, we recommend that the Secretary of the Treasury direct the Fiscal Assistant Secretary, working in coordination with the Controller of OMB's Office of Federal Financial Management, to establish and implement effective procedures for (1) reporting amounts in the CFS budget statements that are fully consistent with the underlying information in significant federal entities' audited financial statements and other financial data and (2) identifying and reporting all items needed to prepare the CFS budget statements.

OMB's FFMIA Reporting Requirement

During our audit of the fiscal year 2012 CFS, we notified OMB of a reporting requirement in OMB Circular No. A-136 that may result in inconsistent and inaccurate reporting of compliance with FFMIA. Under FFMIA, both CFO Act entities[16] and their auditors are required to make an annual determination as to whether an entity's financial management systems[17] substantially comply with (1) federal financial management systems requirements, (2) applicable federal accounting standards, and (3) the *U.S. Standard General Ledger* at the transaction level. Consistent with the act, OMB Circular No. A-136 requires the CFO Act entities to report annually on their determination, as well as their auditors' determination, of compliance with each of the three FFMIA requirements in the Summary of Management Assurances table in their respective annual financial reports or performance and accountability reports. However, the circular also requires the CFO Act entities to report on "overall substantial compliance". The requirement to report such information may create an appearance that the three separate system requirements are not equally important, and result in inconsistent and inaccurate reporting among entities and in the Management's Discussion and Analysis section of the *Financial Report*. In discussions with OMB officials, they stated that OMB plans to resolve the matter by removing the "overall substantial compliance" requirement in connection with OMB's ongoing efforts to revise the circular.

Recommendation for Executive Action

To help assure the consistency and clarity of FFMIA compliance reporting in CFO Act entities' annual financial reports or performance and accountability reports and the Management's Discussion and Analysis section of the *Financial Report*, we recommend that the Director of OMB ensure that OMB continues its efforts to remove the requirement for reporting "overall substantial compliance" from OMB Circular No. A-136, *Financial Reporting Requirements*.

STATUS OF RECOMMENDATIONS FROM PRIOR REPORTS

Of our 48 recommendations from our prior reports regarding control deficiencies in the CFS preparation process that were open at the end of the fiscal year 2011 audit, we closed 17 recommendations during our fiscal year

2012 audit. Of the 17 closed recommendations, we closed 7 as a result of corrective actions taken by Treasury. We closed the other 10 recommendations, which were related to the CFS budget statements, by making 2 new recommendations in this chapter that are better aligned with the current status of the remaining internal control deficiencies associated with the budget statements and that reflect certain actions taken by Treasury. Thirty-one recommendations from our prior reports remained open as of January 9, 2013, the date of our report on the audit of the fiscal year 2012 CFS.

Appendix I summarizes the status as of January 9, 2013, of the 48 open recommendations from our prior years' reports. Specifically, appendix I includes the status according to Treasury and OMB, as well as our own assessments where appropriate. The status of recommendations per GAO includes explanatory comments on Treasury's and OMB's information. We will continue to monitor Treasury's and OMB's progress in addressing our recommendations as part of our fiscal year 2013 CFS audit.

AGENCY COMMENTS AND OUR EVALUATION

OMB Comments

In oral comments on a draft of this chapter, OMB generally concurred with the findings and recommendations in this chapter. OMB also provided technical comments, which were incorporated as appropriate.

Treasury Comments

In written comments on a draft of this chapter, Treasury concurred with four of the five recommendations and stated that it will consider the recommendation related to the restatement and reclassification assessment. We continue to believe that this assessment will help assure the comparability of the CFS between the current and prior fiscal year.

To address the long-standing material weakness related to intragovernmental transactions, Treasury stated that it is continuing to develop the General Fund reporting entity to address the intragovernmental elimination differences that occur when a federal entity records the General Fund as a trading partner. Treasury is also working with federal entities and the audit community to develop and strengthen policy and guidance for reporting of intragovernmental transactions, including a number of measures intended to enhance the identification, resolution, and prevention of intragovernmental imbalances. In addition, Treasury noted that it is continuing its efforts to reconcile the budget deficit to federal entities' audited financial statements for the compilation of the two budget statements included in the CFS.

This chapter contains recommendations to you. The head of a federal agency is required by 31 U.S.C. 720 to submit a written statement on actions taken on our recommendations to the Senate Committee on Homeland Security and Governmental Affairs and to the House Committee on Oversight and Government Reform not later than 60 days after the date of this chapter. A written statement must also be sent to the Senate and House Committees on Appropriations with the agency's first request for appropriations made more than 60 days after the date of this chapter.

We are sending copies of this chapter to interested congressional committees, the Fiscal Assistant Secretary of the Treasury, and the Controller of the Office of Management and Budget's Office of Federal Financial Management.

Gary T. Engel
Director
Financial Management and Assurance

APPENDIX I: STATUS OF TREASURY'S AND OMB'S PROGRESS IN ADDRESSING GAO'S PRIOR YEAR RECOMMENDATIONS FOR PREPARING THE CFS

Count	No.	Recommendation	Status of recommendation[a]	
			Per Treasury and OMB	Per GAO
GAO-04-45(results of the fiscal year 2002 audit)				
1	02-4	As the Department of the Treasury (Treasury) is designing its new financial statement compilation process to begin with the fiscal year 2004 consolidated financial statements of the U.S. government (CFS), the Secretary of the Treasury should direct the Fiscal Assistant Secretary, in coordination with the Controller of the Office of Management and Budget (OMB), to develop reconciliation procedures that will aid in understanding and controlling the net position balance as well as eliminate the plugs previously associated with compiling the CFS.	To eliminate or explain adjustments to net position, Treasury eliminates, at the consolidated level, intragovernmental activity and balances using formal balanced accounting entries (via Reciprocal Categories) and analyzes transactions that contribute to the unmatched transactions and balances adjustment i.e., the plug. Major contributors to the plug are transactions with the General Fund. A Treasury task group has developed the Schedule of General Fund Authority and will enter fiscal year 2013 General Fund data via journal voucher into the Government-wide Financial Report System (GFRS). In the interim, Treasury provides agencies with selected General Fund data on a monthly basis to facilitate reconciliation of agency transactions with the General Fund on a quarterly basis. In addition, Treasury issued new guidance in fiscal year 2013 for recording intragovernmental transactions and for resolving material differences. In addition, throughout fiscal year 2013, Treasury will identify and resolve, via communications to, and assistance from, agencies, material differences related to	Open.

Count	No.	Recommendation	Status of recommendation[a]	
			Per Treasury and OMB	Per GAO
GAO-04-45(results of the fiscal year 2002 audit)				
			fiduciary, benefits, buy/sell, and transfer activity via quarterly metrics and scorecard data to assist the agencies in identifying and mitigating root causes for differences and to implement both short- and long-term solutions.	
2	02-9	The Secretary of the Treasury should direct the Fiscal Assistant Secretary, in coordination with the Controller of OMB, to design procedures that will account for the difference in intragovernmental assets and liabilities throughout the compilation process by means of formal consolidating and elimination accounting entries.	See the status of recommendation No. 02-4.	Open.
3	02-10	The Secretary of the Treasury should direct the Fiscal Assistant Secretary, in coordination with the Controller of OMB, to develop solutions for intragovernmental activity and balance issues relating to federal agencies' accounting, reconciling, and reporting in areas other than those OMB now requires be reconciled, primarily areas relating to appropriations.	See the status of recommendation No. 02-4.	Open.

Appendix I. (Continued)

Count	No.	Recommendation	Status of recommendation[a]	
			Per Treasury and OMB	Per GAO
GAO-04-45(results of the fiscal year 2002 audit)				
4	02-11	The Secretary of the Treasury should direct the Fiscal Assistant Secretary, in coordination with the Controller of OMB, to reconcile the change in intragovernmental assets and liabilities for the fiscal year, including the amount and nature of all changes in intragovernmental assets or liabilities not attributable to cost and revenue activity recognized during the fiscal year. Examples of these differences would include capitalized purchases, such as inventory or equipment, and deferred revenue.	Treasury's consolidating procedures include requests for information from the agencies related to asset capitalization and agency advances or deferred revenue to assist in ensuring the proper reporting of this activity. During fiscal year 2013, Treasury will continue working on guidance related to intragovernmental capitalized purchases that was begun during fiscal year 2012. See the status of recommendation No. 02-4.	Open.
5	02-12	The Secretary of the Treasury should direct the Fiscal Assistant Secretary to develop and implement a process that adequately identifies and reports items needed to reconcile net operating cost and unified budget surplus (or deficit). Treasury should report "net unreconciled	Treasury has taken certain actions regarding the two CFS budget statements to address GAO's past recommendations. Treasury is committed to continuing its efforts to address the remaining control deficiencies in this area.	Closed. Over the past few years, Treasury has taken certain actions to address recommendations related to the two CFS budget statements. To provide recommendations that are better aligned with the remaining control

Count	No.	Recommendation	Status of recommendation[a]	
			Per Treasury and OMB	Per GAO
GAO-04-45(results of the fiscal year 2002 audit)				
		differences" included in the net operating results line item as a separate reconciling activity in the reconciliation statement.		deficiencies in this area, we have (1) closed this recommendation and (2) included in this chapter under "Preparation of the Budget Statements Included in the CFS" new recommendations for corrective action.
6	02-13	The Secretary of the Treasury should direct the Fiscal Assistant Secretary to develop and implement a process that adequately identifies and reports items needed to reconcile net operating cost and unified budget surplus (or deficit). Treasury should develop policies and procedures to ensure completeness of reporting and document how all the applicable components reported in the other consolidated financial statements (and related note disclosures included in the CFS) were properly reflected in the reconciliation statement.	See the status of recommendation No. 02-12.	Closed. Over the past few years, Treasury has taken certain actions to address recommendations related to the two CFS budget statements. To provide recommendations that are better aligned with the remaining control deficiencies in this area, we have (1) closed this recommendation and (2) included in this chapter under "Preparation of the Budget Statements Included in the CFS" new recommendations for corrective action.

Appendix I. (Continued)

Count	No.	Recommendation	Status of recommendation[a]	
			Per Treasury and OMB	Per GAO
GAO-04-45(results of the fiscal year 2002 audit)				
7	02-14	The Secretary of the Treasury should direct the Fiscal Assistant Secretary to develop and implement a process that adequately identifies and reports items needed to reconcile net operating cost and unified budget surplus (or deficit). Treasury should establish reporting materiality thresholds for determining which agency financial statement activities to collect and report at the government-wide level to assist in ensuring that the reconciliation statement is useful and conveys meaningful information.	See the status of recommendation No. 02-12.	Closed. Over the past few years, Treasury has taken certain actions to address recommendations related to the two CFS budget statements. To provide recommendations that are better aligned with the remaining control deficiencies inthis area, we have (1) closed this recommendation and (2) included in this chapter under "Preparation of the Budget Statements Included in the CFS" new recommendations for corrective action.
8	02-15	If Treasury chooses to continue using information from both federal agencies' financial statements and Treasury's central accounting and reporting system (STAR), Treasury should demonstrate how the amounts from	See the status of recommendation No. 02-12.	Closed. Over the past few years, Treasury has taken certain actions to address recommendations related to the two CFS budget statements. To provide recommendations that are

Count	No.	Recommendation	Status of recommendation[a]	
			Per Treasury and OMB	Per GAO
GAO-04-45(results of the fiscal year 2002 audit)				
		STAR reconcile to federal agencies' financial statements.		better aligned with the remaining control deficiencies in this area, we have (1) closed this recommendation and (2) included in this chapter under "Preparation of the Budget Statements Included in the CFS" new recommendations for corrective action.
9	02-16	If Treasury chooses to continue using information from both federal agencies' financial statements and from STAR, Treasury should identify and document the cause of any significant differences, if any are noted.	See the status of recommendation No. 02-12.	Closed. Over the past few years, Treasury has taken certain actions to address recommendations related to the two CFS budget statements. To provide recommendations that are better aligned with the remaining control deficiencies in this area, we have (1) closed this recommendation and (2) included in this chapter under "Preparation of the Budget Statements Included in the CFS" new

Appendix I. (Continued)

Count	No.	Recommendation	Status of recommendation[a]	
			Per Treasury and OMB	Per GAO
GAO-04-45(results of the fiscal year 2002 audit)				
				recommendations for corrective action.
10	02-17	The Secretary of the Treasury should direct the Fiscal Assistant Secretary, in coordination with the Controller of OMB, to develop and implement a process to ensure that the Statement of Changes in Cash Balance from Unified Budget and Other Activities properly reflects the activities reported in federal agencies' audited financial statements. Treasury should document the consistency of the significant line items on this statement to federal agencies' audited financial statements.	See the status of recommendation No. 02-12.	Closed. Over the past few years, Treasury has taken certain actions to address recommendations related to the two CFS budget statements. To provide recommendations that are better aligned with the remaining control deficiencies in this area, we have (1) closed this recommendation and (2) included in this chapter under "Preparation of the Budget Statements Included in the CFS" new recommendations for corrective action.
11	02-20	The Secretary of the Treasury should direct the Fiscal Assistant Secretary, in coordination with the Controller of OMB, to develop and implement a process to ensure that	See the status of recommendation No. 02-12.	Closed. Over the past few years, Treasury has taken certain actions to address recommendations related to the two CFS budget

Count	No.	Recommendation	Status of recommendation[a]	
			Per Treasury and OMB	Per GAO
GAO-04-45(results of the fiscal year 2002 audit)				
		the Statement of Changes in Cash Balance from Unified Budget and Other Activities properly reflects the activities reported in federal agencies' audited financial statements. Treasury should explain and document the differences between the operating revenue amount reported on the Statement of Operations and Changes in Net Position and unified budget receipts reported on the Statement of Changes in Cash Balance from Unified Budget and Other Activities.		statements. To provide recommendations that are better aligned with the remaining control deficiencies inthis area, we have (1) closed this recommendation and (2) included in this chapter under "Preparation of the Budget Statements Included in the CFS" new recommendations for corrective action.
12	02-22	The Secretary of the Treasury should direct the Fiscal Assistant Secretary, in coordination with the Controller of OMB, to perform an assessment to define the reporting entity, including its specific components, in conformity with the criteria issued by the Federal Accounting Standards Advisory Board (FASAB). Key decisions made in this assessment should be documented, including the reason for including or excluding	During fiscal year 2013, Treasury will completely document Treasury's assessment as to whether entities are to be included or excluded in the reporting entity in accordance with the FASAB criteria. As part of this assessment, Treasury will also take into account FASAB's Reporting Entity standard, once it is finalized.	Open.

Appendix I. (Continued)

Count	No.	Recommendation	Status of recommendation[a]	
			Per Treasury and OMB	Per GAO
GAO-04-45(results of the fiscal year 2002 audit)				
		components and the basis for concluding on any issue. Particular emphasis should be placed on demonstrating that any financial information that should be included but is not included is immaterial.		
13	02-23	The Secretary of the Treasury should direct the Fiscal Assistant Secretary, in coordination with the Controller of OMB, to provide in the financial statements all the financial information relevant to the defined reporting entity, in all material respects. Such information would include, for example, the reporting entity's assets, liabilities, and revenues.	During fiscal year 2013, Treasury will work with certain entities that do not currently submit financial statement data to ensure that financial information relevant to the defined reporting entity, in all material respects, is submitted.	Open.
14	02-24	The Secretary of the Treasury should direct the Fiscal Assistant Secretary, in coordination with the Controller of OMB, to disclose in the financial statements all information that is necessary to inform users adequately about the	Pending results of actions taken pursuant to recommendation Nos. 02-22 and 02-23.	Open.

Count	No.	Recommendation	Status of recommendation[a]	
			Per Treasury and OMB	Per GAO
GAO-04-45(results of the fiscal year 2002 audit)				
		reporting entity. Such disclosures should clearly describe the reporting entity and explain the reason for excluding any components that are not included in the defined reporting entity.		
15	02-35	The Secretary of the Treasury should direct the Fiscal Assistant Secretary, in coordination with the Controller of OMB, to help ensure that federal agencies provide adequate information in their legal representation letters regarding the expected outcomes of the cases.	During fiscal year 2013, Treasury will work with the Department of Justice, OMB, and GAO and the agencies to determine if further changes in policy and/or guidance (e.g., OMB Circular A-136) are needed for all agencies to provide the required information regarding the expected outcomes of legal cases in their legal representations.	Open.
16	02-37	The Secretary of the Treasury should direct the Fiscal Assistant Secretary, in coordination with the Controller of OMB, to establish written policies and procedures to help ensure that major treaty and other international agreement information is properly identified and reported in the CFS. Specifically, these policies and procedures should require that federal agencies develop a detailed schedule of all major treaties and	Agencies are currently required to report contingencies in their financial statements and notes pursuant to generally accepted accounting principles (GAAP) guidance. In addition, OMB Circular A-136 specifically references the inclusion of treaties and international agreements within "Commitments and Contingencies." Further, agencies include specific representations with respect to material liabilities or contingencies in their management representations. In addition, the financial statements of most significant entities and many other federal entities received unqualified audit opinions. However, no additional analysis of	Open. Until a comprehensive analysis of major treaty and other international agreement information has been performed, Treasury and OMB are precluded from determining if additional disclosure is required by GAAP in the CFS, and we are precluded from determining whether the

Appendix I. (Continued)

Count	No.	Recommendation	Status of recommendation[a]	
			Per Treasury and OMB	Per GAO
GAO-04-45(results of the fiscal year 2002 audit)				
		other international agreements that obligate the U.S. government to provide cash, goods, or services, or that create other financial arrangements that are contingent on the occurrence or nonoccurrence of future events (a starting point for compiling these data could be the State Department's Treaties in Force).	treaties has been performed to reasonably ensure that all of the federal government's treaties are considered in agency analyses or that agencies are consistently analyzing treaties for recognition or disclosure. Treasury will annually review agency financial statements, audit reports and management representation letters for any references to treaties and international agreements, and if deemed material will disclose in the CFS.	omitted information is material.
17	02-38	The Secretary of the Treasury should direct the Fiscal Assistant Secretary, in coordination with the Controller of OMB, to establish written policies and procedures to help ensure that major treaty and other international agreement information is properly identified and reported in the CFS. Specifically, these policies and procedures should require that federal agencies classify all such scheduled major treaties and other international agreements as commitments or contingencies.	See the status of recommendation No. 02-37.	Open. See the status of recommendation No. 02-37.

Count	No.	Recommendation	Status of recommendation[a]	
			Per Treasury and OMB	Per GAO
GAO-04-45(results of the fiscal year 2002 audit)				
18	02-39	The Secretary of the Treasury should direct the Fiscal Assistant Secretary, in coordination with the Controller of OMB, to establish written policies and procedures to help ensure that major treaty and other international agreement information is properly identified and reported in the CFS. Specifically, these policies and procedures should require that federal agencies disclose in the notes to the CFS amounts for major treaties and other international agreements that have a reasonably possible chance of resulting in a loss or claim as a contingency.	See the status of recommendation No. 02-37.	Open. See the status of recommendation No. 02-37.
19	02-40	The Secretary of the Treasury should direct the Fiscal Assistant Secretary, in coordination with the Controller of OMB, to establish written policies and procedures to help ensure that major treaty and other international agreement information is properly identified and reported in the CFS. Specifically, these policies and	See the status of recommendation No. 02-37.	Open. See the status of recommendation No. 02-37.

Appendix I. (Continued)

Count	No.	Recommendation	Status of recommendation[a]	
			Per Treasury and OMB	Per GAO
GAO-04-45(results of the fiscal year 2002 audit)				
		procedures should require that federal agencies disclose in the notes to the CFS amounts for major treaties and other international agreements that are classified as commitments and that may require measurable future financial obligations.		
20	02-41	The Secretary of the Treasury should direct the Fiscal Assistant Secretary, in coordination with the Controller of OMB, to establish written policies and procedures to help ensure that major treaty and other international agreement information is properly identified and reported in the CFS. Specifically, these policies and procedures should require that federal agencies take steps to prevent major treaties and other international agreements that are classified as remote from being recorded or disclosed as probable or reasonably possible in the CFS.	See the status of recommendation No. 02-37.	Open. See the status of recommendation No. 02-37.

Count	No.	Recommendation	Status of recommendation[a]	
			Per Treasury and OMB	Per GAO
GAO-04-45(results of the fiscal year 2002 audit)				
21	02-129	The Secretary of the Treasury should direct the Fiscal Assistant Secretary to ensure that the note disclosure for stewardship responsibilities related to the risk assumed for federal insurance and guarantee programs meets the requirements of Statement of Federal Financial Accounting Standards No. 5, *Accounting for Liabilities of the Federal Government*, paragraph 106, which requires that when financial information pursuant to Financial Accounting Standards Board standards on federal insurance and guarantee programs conducted by government corporations is incorporated in general purpose financial reports of a larger federal reporting entity, the entity should report as required supplementary information what amounts and periodic change in those amounts would be reported under the "risk assumed" approach.	This information continues to be requested from federal agencies for disclosure in the CFS. Treasury, along with OMB, will work with agencies to improve the consistency of this disclosure in the fiscal year 2013 CFS and will also monitor the work of the FASAB task force that is reviewing the reporting for risk assumed.	Open. Treasury's reporting in this area is not complete. The CFS should include all major federal insurance programs in the risk assumed reporting and analysis. Also, since future events are uncertain, risk assumed information should include indicators of the range of uncertainty around expected estimates, including indicators of the sensitivity of the estimate to changes in major assumptions.

Appendix I. (Continued)

Count	No.	Recommendation	Status of recommendation[a]	
			Per Treasury and OMB	Per GAO
GAO-(results of the fiscal year 2003 audit)				
22	03-6	The Secretary of the Treasury should direct the Fiscal Assistant Secretary to develop a process that will allow full reporting of the changes in cash balance of the U.S. government. Specifically, the process should provide for reporting on the change in cash reported on the consolidated balance sheet, which should be linked to cash balances reported in federal agencies' audited financial statements.	See the status of recommendation No. 02-12.	Closed. Over the past few years, Treasury has taken certain actions to address recommendations related to the two CFS budget statements. To provide recommendations that are better aligned with the remaining control deficiencies in this area, we have (1) closed this recommendation and (2) included in this chapter under "Preparation of the Budget Statements Included in the CFS" new recommendations for corrective action.
23	03-8	The Director of OMB should direct the Controller of OMB, in coordination with Treasury's Fiscal Assistant Secretary, to work with the Department of Justice and certain other executive branch federal agencies to ensure that	During fiscal year 2013, Treasury and OMB will assess options as to what methodologies or approaches to be used for obtaining the additional information needed from the agencies.	Open.

Count	No.	Recommendation	Status of recommendation[a]	
			Per Treasury and OMB	Per GAO
GAO-(results of the fiscal year 2003 audit)				
		these federal agencies report or disclose relevant criminal debt information in conformity with GAAP in their financial statements and have such information subjected to audit.		
24	03-9	The Secretary of the Treasury should direct the Fiscal Assistant Secretary to include relevant criminal debt information in the CFS or document the specific rationale for excluding such information.	See the status of recommendation No. 03-8.	Open.
25	03-11	The Secretary of the Treasury should direct the Fiscal Assistant Secretary, in coordination with the Controller of OMB, to modify Treasury's plans for the new closing package to (1) require federal agencies to directly link their audited financial statement notes to the CFS notes and (2) provide the necessary information to demonstrate that all of the five principal consolidated financial statements are consistent with the	Treasury's current CFS compilation process provides for direct linkage from the 35 significant federal agencies' audited financial statements to most of the CFS principal statements and to the related note disclosures. However, additional work is needed related to the two budgetary financial statements.	Open. Treasury's process for compiling the CFS generally demonstrated that amounts in the Statement of Social Insurance and the Statement of Changes in Social Insurance Amounts were consistent with the underlying federal entities' audited financial statements and that the Balance Sheet and the Statement of Net Cost were also consistent with the 35 significant

Appendix I. (Continued)

Count	No.	Recommendation	Status of recommendation[a]	
			Per Treasury and OMB	Per GAO
GAO-(results of the fiscal year 2003 audit)				
		underlying information in federal agencies' audited financial statements and other financial data.		federal entities' financial statements prior to eliminating intragovernmental activity and balances. However, Treasury's process did not ensure that the information in the remaining three principal financial statements (Statement of Operations and Changes in Net Position, Reconciliation of Net Operating Cost and Unified Budget Deficit, and Statement of Changes in Cash Balance from Unified Budget and Other Activities) was fully consistent with the underlying information in the 35 significant federal entities' audited financial statements and other financial data. With regard

Count	No.	Recommendation	Status of recommendation[a]	
			Per Treasury and OMB	Per GAO
GAO-(results of the fiscal year 2003 audit)				
				to directly linking the last two statements to federal entities' audited financial statements and other financial data, we have incorporated this issue along with other control deficiencies related to the two CFS budget statements into new recommendations for correctiveaction in this chapter under "Preparation of the Budget Statements Included in the CFS."
GAO-05-407 (results of the fiscal year 2004 audit)				
26	04-3	The Secretary of the Treasury should direct the Fiscal Assistant Secretary to require that Treasury employees contact and document communications with federal agencies before recording journal vouchers to change agency audited closing package data.	During fiscal year 2013, Treasury will fully implement and enforce its procedures to document communications with the agencies in the supporting documentation for journal vouchers.	Open.
27	04-6	The Secretary of the Treasury should direct the Fiscal Assistant Secretary to assess the infrastructure associated with the	During fiscal year 2012, Treasury continued to make improvements to its internal control infrastructure. Treasury updated and revised its standard operating procedures (SOP) to document	Open.

Appendix I. (Continued)

Count	No.	Recommendation	Status of recommendation[a]	
			Per Treasury and OMB	Per GAO
GAO-05-407 (results of the fiscal year 2004 audit)				
		compilation process and modify it as necessary to achieve a sound internal control environment.	that key controls are in place at all critical areas of the CFS preparation process. Treasury will monitor and assess its efforts during fiscal year 2013 to determine its progress in achieving a sound internal control environment.	
GAO-07-805(results of the fiscal year 2006 audit)				
28	06-6	The Secretary of the Treasury should direct the Fiscal Assistant Secretary, working in coordination with the Controller of OMB's Office of Federal Financial Management, to establish effective processes and procedures to ensure that appropriate information regarding litigation and claims is included in the government-wide legal representation letter.	Treasury, in coordination with OMB and Justice, will work during fiscal year 2013 to establish effective processes and procedures to require that appropriate information regarding litigation and claims is included in the government-wide legal representation letter.	Open.
29	06-7	The Secretary of the Treasury should direct the Fiscal Assistant Secretary, working in coordination with the Controller of OMB's Office of Federal Financial Management, to develop a process for obtaining sufficient information from federal agencies to enable	The monitoring of intragovernmental differences and their resolution effort is being significantly increased in fiscal year 2013 via quarterly intragovernmental metrics and scorecard meetings with the agencies. This expanded monitoring and resolution effort commenced during the first quarter of fiscal year 2013 and will continue throughout the remaining quarters and at yearend.	Open.

Count	No.	Recommendation	Status of recommendation[a]	
			Per Treasury and OMB	Per GAO
GAO-07-805(results of the fiscal year 2006 audit)				
		Treasury and OMB to adequately monitor federal agencies' efforts to reconcile intragovernmental activity and balances with their trading partners. This information should include (1) the nature and a detailed description of the significant differences that exist between trading partners' records of intragovernmental activity and balances, (2) detailed reasons why such differences exist, (3) details of steps taken or being taken to work with federal agencies' trading partners to resolve the differences, and (4) the potential outcome of such steps.	The agencies will provide corrective actions based on these meetings. Treasury will monitor their corrective actions during the remaining quarters and at yearend with the ultimate goal to reduce intragovernmental differences to an immaterial level. In addition to this expanded monitoring and resolution activity, agencies can seek out further resolution of their differences via a dispute resolution process. See also the status of recommendation No. 02-4.	
GAO-08-748(results of the fiscal year 2007 audit)				
30	07-1	The Secretary of the Treasury should direct the Fiscal Assistant Secretary to enhance and fully document all practices referred to in the SOP entitled "Preparing the Financial Report of the U.S. Government" to better ensure that practices are proper, complete, and	See the status of recommendation No. 02-12.	Closed. Treasury has taken several actions to address this recommendation. To provide recommendations that are better aligned with the current status of remaining deficiencies related to this area, we have (1) closed this

Appendix I. (Continued)

Count	No.	Recommendation	Status of recommendation[a]	
			Per Treasury and OMB	Per GAO
GAO-08-748(results of the fiscal year 2007 audit)				
		can be consistently applied by staff members.		recommendation based on Treasury's significant progress and (2) included in this chapter under "Preparation of the Budget Statements Included in the CFS" new recommendations for corrective actions for the remaining deficiencies.
31	07-5	The Director of OMB should direct the Controller of OMB's Office of Federal Financial Management, in coordination with Treasury's Fiscal Assistant Secretary, to develop formal processes and procedures for identifying and resolving any material differences in distributed offsetting receipt amounts included in the net outlay calculation of federal agencies' Statements of Budgetary Resources and the amounts included in the computation of the budget deficit in the CFS.	See the status of recommendation No. 02-12.	Closed. Over the past few years, Treasury has taken certain actions to address recommendations related to the two CFS budget statements. To provide recommendations that are better aligned with the remaining control deficiencies in this area, we have (1) closed this recommendation and (2) included in this chapter under "Preparation of the Budget Statements

Count	No.	Recommendation	Status of recommendation[a]	
			Per Treasury and OMB	Per GAO
GAO-08-748(results of the fiscal year 2007 audit)				
				Included in the CFS" new recommendations for corrective action.
32	07-9	The Secretary of the Treasury should direct the Fiscal Assistant Secretary, in coordination with the Controller of OMB's Office of Federal Financial Management, to develop and implement effective processes for monitoring and assessing the effectiveness of internal control over the processes used to prepare the CFS.	See the status of recommendation No. 04-6.	Open.
33	07-10	The Secretary of the Treasury should direct the Fiscal Assistant Secretary, working in coordination with the Controller of OMB's Office of Federal Financial Management, to develop and implement alternative solutions to performing almost all of the compilation effort at the end of the year, including obtaining and utilizing interim financial information from federal agencies.	During fiscal year 2012, Treasury obtained and utilized third quarter information from agencies, focusing on key topics and issues to facilitate year-end CFS preparation. Treasury expects to expand the use of third quarter information in fiscal year 2013 to further facilitate year-end compilation.	Open.

Appendix I. (Continued)

Count	No.	Recommendation	Status of recommendation[a]	
			Per Treasury and OMB	Per GAO
GAO-09-387(results of the fiscal year 2008 audit)				
34	08-01	The Secretary of the Treasury should direct the Fiscal Assistant Secretary to design, document, and implement policies and procedures to identify and eliminate intragovernmental payroll tax amounts at the government-wide level when compiling the CFS.	During fiscal year 2013, Treasury will evaluate the adequacy of the payroll tax amounts reported in the Monthly Treasury Statement by discussing the methodology for preparing this amount with the providing agency. If deemed adequate, policies and procedures will be modified to reflect the results of the analysis and document how this amount is identified and used when compiling the CFS.	Open.
35	08-04	The Secretary of the Treasury should direct the Fiscal Assistant Secretary, in coordination with the Controller of OMB, to develop and implement policies and procedures for assessing and documenting, on an annual basis, which entities meet the criteria established for identifying federal entities as significant to the CFS.	During fiscal year 2012, Treasury implemented policies and procedures for assessing and documenting, on an annual basis, which entities meet the criteria established for identifying federal entities as significant to the CFS.	Closed.
GAO-10-757(results of the fiscal year 2009 audit)				
36	09-04	The Secretary of the Treasury should direct the Fiscal Assistant Secretary to develop, implement, and document procedures for identifying, analyzing, compiling, and reporting all significant	During fiscal year 2012, Treasury developed, implemented, and documented procedures for identifying, analyzing, compiling, and reporting all significant accounting policies and related party transactions at the government-wide level.	Closed.

Count	No.	Recommendation	Status of recommendation[a]	
			Per Treasury and OMB	Per GAO
GAO-10-757(results of the fiscal year 2009 audit)				
		accounting policies and related party transactions at the government-wide level.		
37	09-06	The Secretary of the Treasury should direct the Fiscal Assistant Secretary to enhance the SOP entitled "Statement of Social Insurance, Social Insurance Note, and Required Supplementary Information" to implement and document procedures for assuring the accuracy of staff's work related to preparing the social insurance information for the CFS.	In fiscal year 2013, Treasury will fully comply with its enhanced Statement of Social Insurance SOP to document that all the social insurance information in the CFS is consistent with the agencies' social insurance information.	Open. .
38	09-10	The Secretary of the Treasury should direct the Fiscal Assistant Secretary to implement and document procedures for assuring the accuracy of staff's work related to performing analytical procedures.	During fiscal year 2012, Treasury implemented and documented procedures for assuring the accuracy of staff's work related to performing analytical procedures.	Closed.
GAO-12-529(results from the fiscal year 2011 audit)				
39	11-01	The Acting Director of OMB should direct the Controller of OMB to develop and implement written procedures specifying the steps required for effectively	OMB developed and implemented written procedures specifying the OMB review process of the *Financial Report*.	Open. OMB's written procedures state that the Office of Federal Financial Management provides certification that the

Appendix I. (Continued)

Count	No.	Recommendation	Status of recommendation[a]	
			Per Treasury and OMB	Per GAO
GAO-12-529(results from the fiscal year 2011 audit)				
		reviewing and approving the drafts of the *Financial Report of the United States Government (Financial Report)* before they are provided to GAO, to include clear delineation of the review and approval roles and responsibilities of designated appropriate higher-level officials in OMB's Office of Federal Financial Management, including the Controller of OMB.		*Financial Report* was reviewed and approved by OMB management. However, these procedures do not clearly delineate the review and approval roles and responsibilities of designated appropriate higher-level officials, including the Controller of OMB.
40	11-02	The Secretary of the Treasury should direct the Fiscal Assistant Secretary to revise and implement Treasury's procedures related to preparing and reviewing the drafts of the *Financial Report* before they are provided to GAO, to include clear delineation of the review and approval roles and responsibilities of designated appropriate higher-level officials in the Office of the Fiscal Assistant Secretary, including the Fiscal Assistant Secretary.	During fiscal year 2012, Treasury revised and implemented its procedures related to preparing the *Financial Report* before they are provided to GAO, including clear delineation of the review and approval roles and responsibilities of designated appropriate higher-level officials in the Office of the Fiscal Assistant Secretary, including the Fiscal Assistant Secretary.	Closed.

Count	No.	Recommendation	Status of recommendation[a]	
			Per Treasury and OMB	Per GAO
GAO-12-529(results from the fiscal year 2011 audit)				
41	11-03	The Secretary of the Treasury should direct the Fiscal Assistant Secretary, working in coordination with the Controller of OMB, to develop and implement procedures to provide for the active involvement of key federal entity personnel with technical expertise in relatively new areas and more complex areas in the preparation and review process of the *Financial Report*.	During fiscal year 2013, Treasury will identify complex areas needing key federal entity involvement and will obtain their review of the *Financial Report* related to their specific area prior to the completion of the first draft of the report.	Open.
42	11-04	The Secretary of the Treasury should direct the Fiscal Assistant Secretary to establish a mechanism to ensure that Treasury's CFS disclosure checklist is reviewed and approved by the date in Treasury's policies and procedures.	During fiscal year 2012, Treasury established a mechanism to ensure that the CFS disclosure checklist is revised and approved by the date in its policies and procedures.	Closed.
43	11-05	The Secretary of the Treasury should direct the Fiscal Assistant Secretary to revise the SOP to include requirements for using the CFS disclosure checklist to prepare the format draft of the CFS and to update the CFS disclosure	During fiscal year 2013, Treasury will utilize the CFS disclosure checklists for all drafts of the CFS, including the format draft.	Open.

Appendix I. (Continued)

Count	No.	Recommendation	Status of recommendation[a]	
			Per Treasury and OMB	Per GAO
GAO-12-529(results from the fiscal year 2011 audit)				
		checklist as necessary when subsequent drafts of the CFS are prepared.		
44	11-06	The Secretary of the Treasury should direct the Fiscal Assistant Secretary to enhance the SOP entitled "Data Analysis" to include required steps for pursuing any instances where the information provided to Treasury contains indications that financial information provided by federal entities for inclusion in the CFS may not be in conformity with GAAP, particularly with respect to any recent changes in GAAP.	During fiscal year 2012, Treasury enhanced the SOP entitled " Data Analysis" to include required steps for pursuing any instances where the information provided to Treasury contains indications that financial information provided by federal entities for inclusion in the CFS may not be in conformity with GAAP, particularly with respect to any recent changes in GAAP.	Closed.
45	11-07	The Secretary of the Treasury should direct the Fiscal Assistant Secretary to enhance the Intragovernmental Reporting and Analysis System (IRAS) validation procedures, at a minimum, to include specific steps for testing intragovernmental data of the administrator's assigned entity.	During fiscal year 2012, Treasury enhanced the IRAS validation procedures to, among other things, include specific steps for testing intragovernmental data of the administrator's assigned entity.	Closed.

Count	No.	Recommendation	Status of recommendation[a]	
			Per Treasury and OMB	Per GAO
GAO-12-529(results from the fiscal year 2011 audit)				
46	11-08	The Secretary of the Treasury should direct the Fiscal Assistant Secretary to establish a mechanism for ensuring that all steps in the required validation process are completed, documented, and reviewed prior to the distribution of IRAS reports.	During fiscal year 2013, Treasury will complete and document all steps in the required IRAS validation process prior to the distribution of the IRAS reports.	Open.
47	11-09	The Secretary of the Treasury should direct the Fiscal Assistant Secretary, working in coordination with the Controller of OMB, to enhance the SOP entitled "Significant Federal Entities Identification" to include procedures for identifying any entities that become significant to the *Financial Report* during the fiscal year but were not identified as significant in the prior fiscal year.	Treasury will work with OMB to assess an approach for identifying new entities that become significant to the *Financial Report* during the fiscal year.	Open.
48	11-10	The Secretary of the Treasury should direct the Fiscal Assistant Secretary, working in coordination with the Controller of OMB, to enhance the SOP entitled "Significant Federal Entities	Treasury will work with OMB to assess an approach for obtaining timely audited closing packages from these newly identified entities in the fiscal year that they become significant to the Financial Report.	Open.

Appendix I. (Continued)

Count	No.	Recommendation	Status of recommendation[a]	
			Per Treasury and OMB	Per GAO
GAO-12-529(results from the fiscal year 2011 audit)				
		Identification" to include procedures for obtaining audited closing packages from newly identified significant entities in the year they become significant, including timely written notification to newly identified significant entities.		

Source: GAO, Treasury, and OMB.

[a] The status of the recommendations listed in app. I is as of January 9, 2013, the date of our report on the audit of the fiscal year 2012 CFS.

End Notes

[1] GAO, *Financial Audit: U.S. Government's Fiscal Years 2012 and 2011 Consolidated Financial Statements*, GAO-13-271R (Washington, D.C.: Jan. 17, 2013).

[2] The CFS for the fiscal years ended September 30, 2012 and 2011, consist of the Statements of Net Cost; Statements of Operations and Changes in Net Position; Reconciliations of Net Operating Cost and Unified Budget Deficit; Statements of Changes in Cash Balance from Unified Budget and Other Activities; Balance Sheets; 2012, 2011, 2010, 2009, and 2008 Statements of Social Insurance; and 2012 and 2011 Statements of Changes in Social Insurance Amounts, including the related notes to these financial statements.

[3] Because of significant uncertainties, primarily related to the achievement of projected reductions in Medicare cost growth reflected in the 2012, 2011, and 2010 SOSI, we were unable to, and did not, express opinions on the 2012, 2011, and 2010 SOSI as well as on the 2012 and 2011 Statements of Changes in Social Insurance Amounts. We were, however, able to render unqualified opinions on the 2009 and 2008 SOSI. The Statement of Changes in Social Insurance Amounts became a basic financial statement in fiscal year 2011.

[4] As used in this chapter, accrual-based consolidated financial statements refer to all of the consolidated financial statements and notes, except for those related to the SOSI and the Statements of Changes in Social Insurance Amounts.

[5] Our January 2013 report also discussed material weaknesses and scope limitations that did not relate to the process used to prepare the CFS but that also prevented us from expressing an opinion on the federal government's accrual-based consolidated financial statements.

[6] The *2012 Financial Report of the United States Government*, which includes the CFS and our related audit report, was issued by the Department of the Treasury on January 17, 2013, and is available through Treasury's website at http://www.fms.treas.gov/fr/index.html.

[7] The Government Management Reform Act of 1994 has required such reporting, covering the executive branch of government, beginning with financial statements prepared for fiscal year 1997. 31 U.S.C. 331(e). The federal government has elected to include certain financial information on the legislative and judicial branches in the CFS as well.

[8] A material weakness is a deficiency, or combination of deficiencies, in internal control, such that there is a reasonable possibility that a material misstatement of the entity's financial statements will not be prevented, or detected and corrected, on a timely basis. A deficiency in internal control exists when the design or operation of a control does not allow management or employees, in the normal course of performing their assigned functions, to prevent, or detect and correct, misstatements on a timely basis.

[9] GAO, *Management Report: Improvements Needed in Controls over the Preparation of the U.S. Consolidated Financial Statements*, GAO-12-529 (Washington, D.C.: June 27, 2012).

[10] A significant deficiency is a deficiency, or a combination of deficiencies, in internal control that is less severe than a material weakness, yet important enough to merit attention by those charged with governance.

[11] OMB Circular No. A-136, *Financial Reporting Requirements*, revised, August 3, 2012.

[12] Pub. L. No. 104-208, div. A., § 101(f), title VIII, 110 Stat. 3009, 3009-389 (Sept. 30, 1996).

[13] For fiscal year 2012, Treasury defined the significant federal entities as the 24 Chief Financial Officers Act agencies, Export-Import Bank of the United States, Farm Credit System Insurance Corporation, Federal Communications Commission, Federal Deposit Insurance Corporation, National Credit Union Administration, U.S. Postal Service, Pension Benefit Guaranty Corporation, Railroad Retirement Board, Securities and Exchange Commission, Smithsonian Institution, and Tennessee Valley Authority.

[14] For fiscal year 2012, Treasury defined the significant calendar year-end entities as the Farm Credit System Insurance Corporation, Federal Deposit Insurance Corporation, and National Credit Union Administration.

[15] GAO, *Standards for Internal Control in the Federal Government*, GAO/AIMD-00-21.3.1 (Washington, D.C.: November 1999).

[16] CFOs were established under 31 U.S.C. § 901(b) for 24 specific entities that are subject to the CFO Act, as amended: the Departments of Agriculture, Commerce, Defense, Education, Energy, Health and Human Services, Homeland Security, Housing and Urban Development, the Interior, Justice, Labor, State, Transportation, the Treasury, and Veterans Affairs; Environmental Protection Agency; National Aeronautics and Space Administration; Agency for International Development; General Services Administration; National Science Foundation; Nuclear Regulatory Commission; Office of Personnel Management; Small Business Administration; and Social Security Administration.

[17] FFMIA defines financial management systems as the financial systems and the financial portions of mixed systems necessary to support financial management, including automated and manual processes, procedures, controls, data, hardware, software, and support personnel dedicated to the operation and maintenance of system functions. The term mixed system means an information system that supports both financial and nonfinancial functions of the federal government or components thereof.

INDEX

A

B

C

D

E

F

G

H

I

J

L

M

N

O

P

R

S

T

U

V

W